THE
LEADERSHIP
PUSH

Cope wishes you much success

Enjoy!

Bob Ramsey

THE

LEADERSHIP
PUSH

HOW TO MOTIVATE
EXTRAORDINARY PERFORMANCE
FROM ORDINARY WORKERS

BOB RAMSEY
DANIEL RAMSEY

MORGAN LANEY
PUBLISHERS

Morgan Laney Publishers
Troy, IL 62294

For contact please email at support@morganlaneypublishers.com

Book design by Medlar Publishing Solutions Pvt Ltd

Library of Congress Cataloging-in-Publication Data

Ramsey, Bob, Ramsey, Daniel
The leadership push: how to motivate extraordinary performance from ordinary workers ; Bob Ramsey, Daniel Ramsey
p. cm.
1. Employee Motivation — United States. 2. Management — United States. 3. Teams in the Workplace — United States. I. Title.

Publisher's Cataloging-In-Publication Data
(Prepared by The Donohue Group, Inc.)

Names: Ramsey, Bob, 1957– | Ramsey, Daniel, 1985–
Title: The leadership push : how to motivate extraordinary performance from ordinary workers / Bob Ramsey, Daniel Ramsey.
Description: [Troy, Illinois] : Morgan Laney Publishing, [2018] | Includes bibliographical references.
Identifiers: ISBN 9781732169401 (paperback) | ISBN 9781732169418 (ebook)
Subjects: LCSH: Employee motivation. | Leadership. | Teams in the workplace.
Classification: LCC HF5549.5.M63 R36 2018 (print) | LCC HF5549.5.M63 (ebook) | DDC 658.314--dc23

ISBN 978-1-7321694-0-1

A very special thanks to Angela Mann

TABLE OF CONTENTS

Part I: The Leading Attitude

Part II: The Köhler Effect

Part III: The Task Triangle

Part IV: The Social Circle

THE LEADERSHIP PUSH

Introduction

This project began about ten years ago. We were business consultants as well as corporate trainers, working with large, established clients—clients like Adobe, Merck, Sandia National Laboratories, and Bristol Myers-Squibb. At these companies, we observed stable, routine leadership. These institutions had systems in place for everything. And the leaders mostly filled out paperwork and resolved the occasional employee spat. In response, employees worked modestly, always with career aspirations in mind, often getting poached to work for the competition. And we thought that this was how things worked in the business world.

But all of this changed after we picked up a new client. This was an entrepreneurial company, founded in the past decade and rapidly expanding. When we met with members of the company, we observed something incredible. The workers were intensely loyal to the founder/CEO. It was clear they would do anything for him. They worked long hours. They let go of grudges and avoided office politics. They volunteered for the worst, most uncomfortable tasks. It seemed they would run through brick walls for their leader. And the result was a robust, growing company.

This made a big impression on us. What did that entrepreneurial leader have that other leaders lacked? How was he able to motivate his workers to achieve such extraordinary performance? How was he able to push them so successfully?

We reviewed our consulting notes and analyzed our interviews. And we embarked on a journey to unlock this leadership secret—reviewing clinical trials, comparing the biographies of great leaders, and conducting our own leadership surveys. If there was an answer to our questions, then we were going to find it. We would find the secret to unlock the "leadership push."

What's the leadership push? The word tells us that something is moving—either from rest, or to an accelerated speed. It also tells us that something initiated the movement. Something caused it. That's where leadership comes in. When leaders do something to move their employees a little bit faster or a little bit further, that's the push. That's the secret discovered by the entrepreneurial leader. That's how he built a multimillion dollar business from scratch. He pushed his workers to extraordinary performance. He used the leadership push.

When we finally uncovered this secret, something peculiar happened. Business leaders from beyond our network started asking us questions. Lots of questions. They wanted to know the secret, too. How could they motivate their ordinary people to greatness? How could they inspire their everyday workers to run through brick walls? How could they start using the push?

We fielded questions such as the following:

- "I've got an underperforming employee who is being too lazy. How can I motivate him?"
- "There just doesn't seem to be enough talent on our team. How can we win without better workers?"
- "My people respond better to the stick than to the carrot. How can I change that?"

All of their questions began merging into one. We knew that we had touched on a widespread problem. Leaders everywhere struggled to motivate their ordinary workers. And they didn't have time to research and test the best solutions.

After working with hundreds of clients, and poring over thousands of clinical trials, we've developed a solution. For the past three years, we've been helping leaders in all industries— from banking to manufacturing, from healthcare to defense contracting—to motivate their ordinary employees to accomplish remarkable things.

This book is the result of that journey.

OVERVIEW

The purpose of this book is to explore the subject of employee motivation—specifically, to investigate how to motivate ordinary people to achieve extraordinary performance. This shines a light on three themes: leadership, extraordinary performance, and ordinary people. And as the book progresses, we will define and explore each of these topics. But for now, we will put it plainly. This book is about getting your average workers to work harder. It's about moving your employees out of the ordinary and into the extraordinary.

The structure of this book is simple. It's laid out in four sequential parts, each of which logically builds on the last. Part I is about developing a leader's attitude. Part II is about how to motivate employees to achieve extraordinary performance. Part III is about delegating important tasks. And Part IV is about building a team. Together they form a strategy for the leadership push. To understand this better, let's look briefly at each part.

Part I is about the proper attitude of leadership. You can't motivate people with the wrong attitude. Your people are not robots. They don't just respond to your commands. They pick up on your thoughts. They respond to how you feel. For example, if you hate your team, then it's going to be really difficult to motivate them. You can say all the right words and do all the right things, but your hate is going to bleed through those words and actions. And that will completely undermine your motivational efforts. So before you do anything else, you need to develop the right mindset. Of course, you're free to have any attitude towards someone that you want. But to be an extraordinary leader, there's a particular attitude that you must adopt. Part I will help you both to identify it and achieve it.

Part II answers the motivation riddle. How do you motivate ordinary people to give extraordinary performances? You make them feel like important members of the team. We will make a counterintuitive argument, that ordinary people work harder for others than they do for themselves. These motivational gains require two crucial steps. First, you need to delegate important, meaningful jobs. Then, you need to build a great team. Together, these will make your workers feel essential to the team. And if you can achieve this, your workers will run through brick walls for you. In this section we introduce a model—Köhler's Cone—that will guide us through the rest of the book.

Part III is about the first half of Köhler's Cone: the Task Triangle. The Task Triangle is about elevating a worker's feeling of task importance. People need to know that their jobs matter. They need to know that they are important. And it's your job to convince them that they are. This means you need to delegate tasks correctly, giving people the right tasks with the right style. If you make errors doing this, then you can diminish their feelings of importance. In Part III, we explore communication strategies to use before, during, and after the initial moment of delegation. These techniques combine to increase the importance of the task in a worker's mind. This is the first half of Köhler's Cone.

Part IV is about the second half of Köhler's Cone: the Social Circle. The Social Circle is about making people feel like members of the team. It's about the principles of team building and about the common obstacles that leaders face. We explore the strange influence that teamwork has on performance and the techniques you can use to encourage that sense of social belonging. We also explore and identify the most disastrous mistake that you should avoid—something that can turn a team against you in the most difficult times. Together, these strategies build a strong atmosphere of camaraderie. This is the second half of Köhler's Cone.

These four parts build on each other. First, you learn how to get the attitude of leadership. Then we give you the secret to motivating others, the leadership push. Finally, you perfect the techniques to fulfill both of its motivational requirements. In this way, the book is best if read from start to finish. However, we've designed each chapter to have value on its own. So if you open the book randomly to look for inspiration, you will likely find it.

In each chapter, we will explore anecdotes, clinical research studies, and true stories that we have gathered during our years in the field. We keep things exciting and fast-paced. You won't get bogged down in an overly dense chapter. We keep things light and snappy. We want this book to be valuable for you. We want you to read it. Therefore we've placed a large emphasis on readability.

At the end of each chapter, you will find two things. The first is a chapter summary, presented as bulleted points. This will help you organize the content and refer to it quickly in the future. After the chapter summary, you will find a box of action items. This is the interactive section. It contains work-book-style prompts to apply the content of the chapter to your particular circumstances. The degree to which you implement these action items will greatly affect the success you will have as a result of reading this book. Not only do these items provide an opportunity for active learning—which drives the material into your long-term memory—they also provide you with an invaluable game plan. You will develop strategies and conversational scripts that you can implement immediately. This is where your life will begin to change. If you want to get the most out of this book, do the action items. This is, by far, the most important takeaway of the book.

After reading this book and completing the action items, you will be a better leader. You will have the skills to elicit extraordinary performance from your ordinary workers. You will see your workers and appreciate them for who they are. You will understand the secret of motivation and how to execute it. And you will have a complete game plan of action items, guiding you to apply your knowledge and immediately start leading your people to greatness.

Not only will this help your team win, but it will also help you to accomplish great things in your career. The sky is the limit for a leader who successfully motivates ordinary people. And when you master this skill of motivation—this leadership push—you will be able to achieve the impossible.

This is where our book begins.

PART I

THE LEADING ATTITUDE

CHAPTER 1

THE MIRACLE AT KETTLE HILL

Achieving the Impossible through Leadership

A s a business leader, your job is to motivate people to take action.

On the slowest of days, you need your people to execute their tasks reliably. But in the face of routine and burnout, they might lose momentum. When this happens, you need to motivate people to make the minimum effort required to keep the operation running. If the operation breaks down, then the whole organization will unravel. It's the leader's job to make sure this doesn't happen. As the leader, you must motivate your team members to show up and do their work.

But on some occasions, the minimum requirements of effort won't suffice. Sometimes you need to push your people to give more. Anything less will result in failure. Your team faces a do-or-die situation. And you either lead your people to greatness, or you all go down in flames.

Take, as an example, Teddy Roosevelt. His team faced a do-or-die situation at the end of the nineteenth century. He needed to inspire his people to make extraordinary effort. And if he couldn't push them to greatness, then his illustrious career would be over before it had ever started.

It was the summer of 1898, and the United States and Spain were at war.[1] Roosevelt, who was then assistant secretary to the navy, resigned his post and joined the war effort. He was assigned to the First Volunteer Calvary Division, a unit forever after referred to as the "Rough Riders." Roosevelt personally recruited his volunteer soldiers and trained them for battle. But there wasn't much time. The situation was urgent. The war was happening quickly. So after only a few weeks of military training, the Rough Riders boarded a ship and sailed to Cuba, to engage the Spanish forces in combat.

Once they had landed in Cuba, they started marching inland immediately—into the jungles and towards the action. For over a week, they fought their way through Spanish resistance before finally approaching the region of San Juan Heights. Here was the strategic high ground of Kettle Hill. The Spanish had erected stiff defensive lines at the top, giving themselves a tactical advantage. And from this position, they rained down gunfire onto Roosevelt's division. Caught at the bottom, the Rough Riders were taking heavy losses. Unless they moved, the barrage of Spanish bullets would cut them all down. As the ranking officer on the field, Roosevelt surveyed the situation.

He had two choices. On the one hand, he could order his men back into a more defensive posture, sheltering them from the bullets, but allowing the Spanish to reinforce their strategic advantage. On the other hand, he could order his men to move forward, up the hill, into the bullets, and rush the enemy head-on. If they took the hill now, before it was reinforced, even if lives were lost, then they might save more lives later. It was a harrowing moment. Lives were on the line. But Teddy Roosevelt made a decision. He ordered his Rough Riders to charge the hill, straight into the screaming bullets, with the goal to overrun the Spanish defenses.

Let's consider the Rough Riders' circumstances for a moment. First of all, the situation was difficult. His regiment was overtired and undersupplied. They were a cavalry regiment without horses, having brought only the officer's horses, leaving the rest behind in Florida. And they were exhausted from endless marching. They had marched ceaselessly since making landfall a week before. And now they all suffered from sleep deprivation.

Perhaps their hunger kept them awake. Since the beginning, their rations had been insufficient. The whirlwind campaign had overwhelmed their supply lines. And the past week of near-starvation had drained their energy, slowing their movements. Furthermore, they suffocated in the heat of a subtropical Cuban summer. And now illness was sweeping through the camp. Everyone was miserable. They were fighting a foreign foe in a distant land. It would have been very natural for the Rough Riders to lose motivation as the weeks of agony dragged on.

In addition, let's not forget that Roosevelt's men were not regular army soldiers. They were a volunteer regiment. They were a gang of gamblers, outlaws, cowboys, miners, and big-game hunters that Roosevelt had personally recruited. They had neither the training nor the discipline of battle-hardened, regular troops. This is why they were called "Rough Riders." They weren't polished or sharp. They were rough around the edges. And furthermore, this motley crew had only known each other for a few weeks. But that was all that Roosevelt had.

In this moment, Roosevelt required extraordinary performance from his crew. Charging a hill is not a situation where "easy does it" gets it done. It's a moment when you must put it all on the line. If the Rough Riders gave a less-than-outstanding performance, they would all die.

And Teddy Roosevelt knew this full well. He knew the risks that he and his men were taking. Later he would write, "On the day of the big fight I had to ask my men to do a deed that European military writers consider utterly impossible of performance, that is, to attack over open ground an unshaken infantry armed with the best modern repeating rifles behind a formidable system of entrenchments."[2]

The Rough Riders were a group of ragtag, misfit soldiers and they had to give the performance of their lives against valiant, patriotic, battle-hardened Spaniards—men who were proud of their empire and fighting fiercely to defend it. And now, at their lowest moment, after the elements had all but depleted them, Roosevelt was asking his team to charge into certain death, up a long hill and straight into range of the steady Spanish rifles.

But despite the dangers, Roosevelt believed that his men could win the battle. He ordered the assault and personally led the charge up Kettle Hill. According to the famous war correspondent Richard Harding Davis, "No man who saw Roosevelt take that ride expected he would finish it alive."[3]

As the man on horseback who led the charge, Roosevelt was the primary target for the Spanish. And sure enough, while riding, a bullet struck his horse, making them both fall into barbed wire. So Roosevelt dismounted and surveyed the scene. Members of his regiment were dropping all around him. He could have easily remained with his horse, hunkering down behind it and using it as shelter from the gunfire. He could have picked his moment to reengage carefully, perhaps letting the bulk of his regiment pass him by, and then rejoining the charge from the rear. But he didn't. Instead, he kept charging. With all of his strength—with all of the adrenaline pumping through his veins, and his pistol firing towards the crest of the hill—he kept running towards the goal.

The defensive lines broke! And after a brief firefight at the summit, the Spanish forces retreated. At the top of the hill, while still struggling to catch his breath, Roosevelt looked around and saw something remarkable. His Rough Riders were all around him! They had followed his charge and overrun the Spanish defenses. He could not have taken the hill by himself. He would have died within seconds. But because his team gave him an extraordinary performance, they had all conquered Kettle Hill together.

This success allowed the Americans to push forward and initiate the Siege of Santiago. And by August 13th, the war was over. It was total victory for the Americans—not just for the nation but for Teddy Roosevelt as well. The charge up Kettle Hill catapulted him and the Rough Riders into national fame. The United States awarded Roosevelt with the Medal of Honor for his bravery, making him the only American to win both a Nobel Peace Prize and a Medal of Honor. The fame from this victory would lead him to become the governor of New York, and eventually the president of the United States.

But despite all of this success, he still looked back on the Spanish-American War as the most significant moment in his life. He called this charge up Kettle Hill his "crowded hour." It was a moment when so much happened, in such a short period, that changed so much about his future. In his own mind, it was the defining moment of his life.[4]

So if this was the most critical moment in his life, how was he able to achieve it? After all, he faced many obstacles in this battle. His situation wasn't ideal in any way. He didn't have the best troops, the best supplies, or the most favorable conditions. The odds were against him. And yet he still was successful. How? How did he inspire such extraordinary performance from his regiment?

He forged ahead despite imperfection. He didn't have time to wait for perfect circumstances. Events were unfolding all around him. If he were to achieve greatness, then he would have to do so with the people he had, not with the people he wanted. And so he was determined to lead with all his might, despite the limitations.

This attitude of leadership allowed him to win a life-changing victory for his nation, for his men, and for himself.

CHAPTER SUMMARY

- Your attitude makes a big difference to your leadership ability.
- Great leaders can achieve remarkable things.
- If you take the actions of great leadership, then you can achieve large goals.

ACTION ITEMS

- Brainstorm five huge leadership goals that you would like to accomplish (for example, "get promoted to regional director in two years.").

1. _____

_____

2. _____

_____

3. _____

_____

4. _____

_____

5. _____

_____

- List five resources or advantages that you currently have that can help you accomplish your goals (for example, "We have a team with a combined fifty years of experience in this industry.").

  1. _____

  _____

  2. _____

  _____

  3. _____

  _____

  4. _____

  _____

  5. _____

  _____

- List three emotions that you will feel after accomplishing your largest, most exciting leadership goal (for example, "unshakeable self-esteem and self-importance").

  1. _____

  _____

  2. _____

  _____

  3. _____

  _____

CHAPTER 2

NOBODY IS COMING

Taking Responsibility for Results

Your situation is probably not much different than Teddy Roosevelt's was when he stood at the base of Kettle Hill.

You probably have a big goal or dream that you want to accomplish. Maybe it's securing a promotion or a big sale. Maybe you are trying to build a company or run for office. Maybe you dream of becoming a champion ice hockey player and winning the Stanley Cup. Whatever your ambition may be, you probably have one that, if you achieved it, would drastically improve your life. For Roosevelt, it was the taking of Kettle Hill and ascending to the presidency. That was his dream. But we all have one—including you.

And maybe you are similar to Teddy Roosevelt in that your goal involves other people. After all, Roosevelt couldn't take Kettle Hill by himself. If he had run up alone, then he would have died. He needed a group of soldiers to follow him up, to bring the firepower and to overwhelm the defenses. Simply put, he needed the performance of others. The *extraordinary* performance of others.

Maybe you lead a team or run an organization. Maybe the big goals you want to achieve require the excellent performance of other people. Anybody who depends on employees, teammates, or suppliers knows this feeling. A chef can cook the best meal in the world, but if the waitstaff is rude, then customers will be dissatisfied. An inventor can develop a groundbreaking product, but that effort is all for nothing if the venture capitalists break their promises. The best basketball player in the world cannot accomplish much unless his teammates also perform well. Some projects depend on the performance of other people. Chances are that your project does, too.

And, maybe like the Rough Riders, the people on your team aren't exactly superstars. Maybe they are a group of imperfect misfits. People from diverse backgrounds with differing skills. People who get emotional. People with petty quirks that grind against the wheels of efficiency. And maybe you're losing hope that these people can help you achieve greatness. Maybe you're worried that these people are holding you back, and that you won't reach that goal until you get some new people on the team.

This fear is common.

Several years ago, we had a consultation with the executives of a midsize energy company. After one meeting, we stayed behind with one of the executives and discussed growth strategies. He told us about a vast region of Oklahoma that was currently untapped and wide open for the taking. It was low-hanging fruit—the kind that can yield enormous profits. His eyes lit up as he described it. If his company could break into that region, then they would have almost no competition, he said. And they would add millions upon millions to their bottom line. But then the brightness faded from his face. "We just don't have the people," he sighed. "We have the money, we have the resources and we have the technology. We just don't have the people…" Of course, he already had people. But he was pinning his hopes on having a new, better group of people to lead. But they never showed up. Like Teddy Roosevelt, he wouldn't achieve success unless he could figure out how to lead the people he already had.

For the past several years, we have hosted and facilitated an executive roundtable where business owners and CEOs from different industries come together to discuss and solve their business problems. Industries that are represented include finance, defense contracting, manufacturing, and energy. In 2018, we surveyed these CEOs about their forecasts and concerns for the following year.[5] And here's something interesting that we discovered: as a whole, they rated the "availability of key skills" as the single largest concern. Think about that. Their primary concern was that they didn't have the right people. And it seemed that the bar concerning team members' skills was continually being raised. Elsewhere in the survey, we asked them about their talent management processes. And the vast majority—83 percent—said that they were looking for "a much broader range of skills when hiring than they did in the past." Clearly, leaders perceived a lack of talent on their existing teams.

We've seen firsthand how widespread a concern this still is. Almost all leaders, somewhere deep in their hearts, have wished for better people. Many recite the timeworn bromide that "their people are their greatest source of competitive advantage." The problem is, they don't actually *feel* that they have much of an advantage. They feel competitive pressures closing in all around them. And so they come to the hesitant conclusion that their weak competitive advantage must be because they lack strong people!

And so they start blaming the other people on their team. This happens in business, in families, in churches, on sports teams, and in community groups of all kinds. Leaders dream of lofty goals but feel handicapped by their team. And so they fantasize about a different team for them to lead—a team of superstars, where there will be no problems and everyone will be overqualified. And they wish that somehow, some way, these new people would just sweep in and carry everyone to victory.

But nobody is coming.

If you wait for the perfect people to come along, then you will wait forever. And you will squander the opportunities that you have right now. Remember Teddy Roosevelt. The Spanish-American War was happening with or without him. He didn't have time to wait until he had a squadron of perfect soldiers. He had to seize the opportunity with his volunteers. And that's what you need to do, too. You need to use the people you have to accomplish the extraordinary achievements that no one thought were possible. As Roosevelt said, if you want to be successful, "Do what you can, with what you have, where you are." And nowhere is this truer than in leadership. The slogan for every leader should be, "Lead the people you can, with what you have, wherever you are." Because if you wait for someone better to come along, then you're going to be waiting for your whole career.

There's a famous story that illustrates this dynamic. It's one of the most famous stories in professional speaking, coming from one of the original motivational speeches. The story is called "Acres of Diamonds," and it was told hundreds of times to fund Temple University in the late nineteenth century.[6]

The story goes like this: There was a landowner in a small town who felt he was down on his luck. But he had big dreams to build a fortune. He had heard stories of people who had discovered diamonds in faraway lands and become fabulously wealthy. So he sold his property and spent the next decade searching for diamonds in foreign soil. But he found nothing. He struggled in poverty. And after wasting years of his life, he returned to his small village. But there he saw something shocking. The new owner of his land had become fabulously wealthy! Asking the villagers, he learned that the new landowner had grown rich after discovering a colossal vein of diamonds on the land that used to be his. So when the original landowner had felt frustrated and dreamed of diamonds in faraway lands, he had actually been sitting on acres of diamonds all along.

Let's apply this lesson to leadership. Many leaders are like that landowner. They dream of success and are willing to do anything to achieve it. But they don't believe that they currently have the resources to achieve it. They don't believe that they have the right people. So they grow frustrated. And they take one of two paths: either they leave seeking greener pastures, on an endless journey to find the perfect team, or they sink into their cynicism and bitterly scrape out a living. In either case, they never achieve their goals.

But what is the story telling us? There are acres of diamonds right underneath our feet! Exactly where we are! We can achieve all of the success we need by using the people and the resources that we already have. We just need the right leadership skills—the skills to bring up the diamonds that no one else can see. The story tells us that the grass isn't greener on the other side—it is green where you water it. It's green where you *work*. So if you want to achieve your goals, you need to water your grass—that is, you need to start doing a better job of leading the people that you already have.

Now let's face reality: it's more exciting to travel the world than to dig for diamonds in your own backyard. But nothing is more rewarding than a big success or life-changing achievement.

And, like the landowner in the story learned, you'll be much happier if you achieve a big success right where your are than no success in an exotic locale.

And let's also recognize that this is the kind of leadership that the world needs. Think about it. There's no great skill in leading perfect people, is there? Perfect people can practically lead themselves. If anyone tells you that the secret to leadership is to surround yourself with perfect people, then they haven't been responsible for their own success. They just, as Ralph Waldo Emerson put it, merely hitched their wagon to an already rising star! And here's the reality: there's no shortage of people willing to hitch their wagon to a rising star. But the world is *desperate* for leaders who can take an average group of people and help them achieve extraordinary things. Those are the leaders that can turn a company around or build a world-class organization. And that's the leadership that people crave.

Furthermore, being that kind of leader is your best chance to move up the corporate ladder. To illustrate this, let's imagine someone named Stacey. Stacey works as a middle manager and wants to get promoted. But the team she leads is full of imperfect, ordinary people. Now what's the best way for her to get a promotion? Is it by complaining to her boss that she needs new people— that she can't achieve success with her current team? Probably not. It's difficult to get ahead while you're making excuses. But what if, instead, Stacey fully committed to her team? What if she found a way to get them to perform better and achieve success, despite the challenges? Whom would you rather promote? The leader who blames her team for her lack of success? Or the leader who succeeds *despite* having imperfect people?

Most CEOs we know would hesitate to promote the first leader. Why? Because if Stacey can't motivate people on her current team, then why would she be able to do so with a more important team? Why trust her when the stakes are high if you couldn't trust her when the stakes are low? In contrast, they would be eager to promote the second leader. "If Stacey had success with those misfits," they reason, "just imagine what she could accomplish with seasoned winners!" Ask yourself this: which reputation would you rather have with your CEO? Your upward mobility depends on how you answer. You need to be a leader who succeeds despite the difficulties, rather than gets sidelined by them.

If you want to achieve your big goal—to have your big moment—then you must accept the simple reality: Nobody is coming. Nobody is coming to save you. And nobody is coming to replace your motley, flawed team with all-stars. If you have imperfect people now, then you will probably be working with these same imperfect people for the foreseeable future. And you have a simple choice: You can either complain about your people and let your possible achievements slip away, or you can be proactive. You can take responsibility for your situation and lead your imperfect people on to great success. Because with the right leadership, great success can come to even the most flawed team members. Even the Rough Riders can win the battle.

CHAPTER SUMMARY

- Many leaders mistakenly wait for better people to come along, but nobody is coming.
- If you search for diamonds in foreign lands, then you will miss the opportunities right where you are.
- It takes no skill to lead perfect people, therefore you deserve no reward for leading them.

- You won't become a great leader until you take personal responsibility for your team's results.

ACTION ITEMS

- Honestly rate your current leadership attitude (1 = hold out for new people, 10 = try to succeed with current team)

_____

- Identify three circumstances that make you feel powerless (for example, when human resources vetoes a potential hire that you requested).

1. _____

   _____

2. _____

   _____

3. _____

   _____

- List five ways to remind yourself that you are responsible for success (for example, place a Post-it note on your bathroom mirror that says, "If it's to be, it's up to me!").

1. _____

   _____

2. _____

   _____

3. _____

_____

4. _____

_____

5. _____

_____

CHAPTER 3

SIC PARVIS MAGNA

Embracing Untapped Potential

L eadership requires a particular attitude. And it's an attitude that most people will never understand. It reflects an element of reality that most would-be leaders simply don't recognize. And it's this omission that lies at the root of their failure.

To understand this attitude, let's travel back to the Caribbean in the late sixteenth century. Once again, the mighty Spanish empire was controlling the Americas and funneling vast amounts of gold back to Europe. But this time, Spain was in conflict, not with America, but with Elizabethan England. And the man at the center of this dispute was Sir Francis Drake.[7]

Drake was born into obscurity. Because of religious persecution, the Drake family was forced to leave the town where Francis was born and move to the coast of England. He was a child without any clear future path. But he was a hard worker. And as a boy, he apprenticed under a local merchant who transported goods across the English Channel. Drake worked hard, making the most of this opportunity. And then the unexpected happened: the shipmaster died. And, having no heirs, he had bequeathed the ship to young Drake. And thus began a life of adventure and achievement that no one could have foreseen.

Drake sailed across the Atlantic several times before the age of twenty-seven—this in the 1560s when the risk of being at sea was incredibly high. And then he began harassing the Spanish, plundering their ships and stealing their treasure. This was done in the interests of the English, who had a rivalry with Spain. It served the Crown to weaken the Spanish shipping operations. But the English didn't supply Drake with the newest ships or elite seaman. Instead, Drake had to lead a crew of motley sea dogs—untamed, unmannered men, drawn to the lawlessness of the open ocean and always a single irritation away from downright mutiny.

But Drake didn't let the flaws of his crew deter him. In 1573, while raiding land operations in Panama, he and his crew plundered a Spanish mule train and stole twenty tons of gold and silver. This was a huge heist—more than they expected and too much for them to carry away all at once. But when he and his raiding crew went to find their transport ships, they were gone— disappeared back up the coast! So Drake and his men were stranded in enemy territory. If discovered, they could expect to be drawn and quartered. And every passing minute brought that fate closer to being realized. But Drake wasn't ready to give up. So he rallied his small band of men. They buried the treasure and built a makeshift raft from materials they found on the beach. Then they used it to sail ten miles up the coast, through treacherous waters, back to their flagship. Later, they returned to recover the treasure. His old salty seamen had come through for him. And he built a reputation through such adventures. To the Spanish, he was a pirate—and certainly, he committed his fair share of sins against them. But to the English, he became a hero.[8]

In 1577, Drake raised enough money for the grandest adventure of all: a circumnavigation of the globe. Only Magellan had completed the task before. And for most, the voyage would mean certain death. But Drake would not be deterred. He caught a full gust of wind and sailed fearlessly into the horizon. And although he and his crew defended themselves against savage attacks by tribesman at the tip of South America, he kept sailing. Though they encountered enemy ships off the coast of Peru, who fought them and plundered their ship, causing them to sustain heavy losses so far from home, he kept sailing. Though their ship was ripped open by an exposed reef in Indonesia, he found a way to keep sailing. And after three long years of savage dangers and constant threats, he became the first Englishman to have sailed around the globe, putting him in the ranks of the most celebrated explorers in the world. All of this notoriety would reach an apex eight years later when Drake led the Royal Navy to defeat the mighty Spanish Armada at the Battle of Gravelines. As a result he would be forever enshrined in the pantheon of English heroes.

This service to the English Crown came with the honor of knighthood. And he was officially knighted by Queen Elizabeth I herself. Forever after, this young, impoverished boy who had dreamed of adventure would be known to history as Sir Francis Drake. He had come from obscurity to achieve more as an English seaman than anyone had before him.

Drake came from a humble background. His family didn't have a coat of arms or a heraldic motto. So Queen Elizabeth christened him with a new motto: "Sic Parvis Magna." This Latin phrase translates into something like, "Greatness from small beginnings" or, "Great things coming from small things." And didn't Drake's own life confirm this? An unremarkable boy grew to gain the great favor of the Queen of England? Don't be surprised...Sic Parvis Magna. Drake used a group of motley, ill-trained pirates to plunder the riches of well-trained sailors? That's how life goes...Sic Parvis Magna. A wayward buccaneer one day defeated the mighty Spanish Armada? Sic Parvis Magna. Greatness comes from small beginnings.

Why is this story so important to leadership? Leaders need to remember that greatness doesn't only come from proven winners, fancy resumés, and Ivy League schools. Greatness comes from average people, too. Teddy Roosevelt took Kettle Hill with a group of misfits. Drake plundered the Spanish with a ragtag team of salty pirates. You don't need an elite group of people to achieve great things. Sic Parvis Magna. You can achieve the extraordinary with the most ordinary people.

Consider the acorn. It's small, and looks very ordinary. But, under the right conditions, it can grow into an oak—one of the strongest and most stately of trees. Now here's what you need to do as a leader: you need to be able to look at the acorn and see the tree, even though it isn't yet a tree. You need to look at your ordinary people and see their potential—and you need to realize that your job as a leader is to bring it out. Don't look at a handful of acorns and curse them because they are only small seeds. That's what ordinary people do, but not great leaders. As a leader, you need to plant the acorns, tend to them, and help them to grow. Why? Because greatness comes from small things. And it's your actions as a leader that will unlock this greatness.

Your role needs to be very much like that of a gardener. Just because a peach tree is small now doesn't mean that it will be small forever. Just because it isn't bearing fruit now doesn't mean that it will never bear fruit in the future. But it takes a gardener to elicit the fruit from a young and fragile tree. Anyone can pick the fruit off of an established, fruit-bearing peach tree. That's not impressive. But the act of caretaking it—of nourishing and nurturing it—is the work of an artist. That is the work of a leader! To look at young trees with no leaves or fruit and see the potential greatness in it. To remember that Sic Parvis Magna and that, with a little work, this orchard can one day be highly productive. That is a gardener's work. And if you want to be a great leader, then it must be your work, too.

And keep this in mind: Sic Parvis Magna applies to you, too, not just the members of your team. Maybe you haven't been the best leader in the past. Maybe you've made gross errors that continue to haunt you. It doesn't matter. Sic Parvis Magna. Greatness comes from small beginnings—from imperfect beginnings. It's not too late for you to achieve greatness. All you have to do is practice the skills of leadership. Use the leadership push and the people around you will respond. You will be able to elicit greatness from them, and with that greatness you can achieve victories that you never before thought possible. And it all starts with your attitude.

CHAPTER SUMMARY

- Great things come from small beginnings.
- Your workers can achieve great things now, even if they haven't in the past.
- Leaders need the attitude of a gardener, realizing the potential of a barren orchard.
- You can become a great leader, even if you've made mistakes in the past.

ACTION ITEMS

- Identify three instances when you have personally witnessed great things coming from small beginnings (for example, "An immigrant neighbor of mine was born into poverty but went on to medical school and eventually became the the chief of surgery at the hospital.").

1. _____

_____

2. _____

_____

3. _____

_____

- Write a list of five scripts that reflect a Sic Parvis Magna attitude (for example, "When I look at this team, all I see is potential. It doesn't matter where we've been—together we can accomplish amazing things!").

1. _____

_____

2. _____

_____

3. _____

_____

4. _____

_____

5. _____

_____

- List three ways that you can succeed despite having an imperfect past (for example, "Even though I was at the helm for a two-year fall in profits, I can still make this branch the most profitable in the company!").

1. _____

_____

2. _____

_____

3. _____

_____

CHAPTER 4

THE BUFFALO DANCE

Revering Your Source Material

This book is about how to achieve your big goals under less-than-ideal circumstances. It's about leading the team you actually have, not the team you wish you had. And it's about how to lead that team to extraordinary performance.

This scope gives us three elements: leadership, extraordinary performance, and ordinary people. And these three themes run throughout the whole book. Together, they form the overarching focus. So let's look at each one of these elements individually.

The first element of this book is leadership. Leadership is all about accomplishing tasks with—and through—other people. Sure, you can achieve some accomplishments alone, but this book is for those that require other people.

An excellent example of working alone comes from Grigori Perelman. On his own, Perelman solved a monumental mathematical problem, proving the Poincaré conjecture. This achievement was so significant that in 2006 he won the Fields Medal—the mathematical equivalent of the Nobel Prize. And in 2010, he won a Millennium Prize from the Clay Mathematics Institute, which included a $1 million reward—although he was so uninterested in social achievement that he declined both awards.[9]

This indicates something significant. He achieved his mathematical breakthrough and his proof alone. Did he learn from others along the way? Certainly! Did he stand on the shoulders of giants? Of course! But to prove the theorem, he ultimately sat down alone with a pencil and paper and put his hand to his forehead. It was a solo job. Some projects are like that. They just require the work of a single mind or of a single set of hands. And that's okay! These are still great achievements! But that way of working is not our focus in this book.

Perelman didn't need a team of people to write his mathematical proof, but Teddy Roosevelt needed a team to charge up Kettle Hill. And what Roosevelt did is where our interest lies. We're looking at projects that require performance from other people—projects requiring teamwork, as well as someone to lead that team. That's leadership.

An example of a different type of leadership than Roosevelt's is a common brand of impersonal "leadership." This is the kind of activity where a person sits behind a desk and makes policy decisions that affect the masses. For example, a CEO might decide to upgrade all of the lights in his factory to LED bulbs. That would lower the energy bill and dramatically alter the working conditions in the factory. And this could potentially make a big difference to the company's success. But that kind of leadership is not our current focus.

Our interest is in the personal, face-to-face interaction that can inspire people to greater performance. The kind of leadership that happens between and among people. It's tempting for leaders to try to solve all of their problems by tweaking policy. But that's not leadership. That's administration. And that's not our focus.

Our focus is leadership. Leadership inspires people to stand up and fight. Leadership motivates people to charge a hill into a hail of gunfire. Policy can't inspire that. Bureaucrats can't achieve that. This book is not a blueprint for bureaucrats. It's a game plan for people who want to *lead*—who want to personally push their people to higher performance. It's about those leadership functions that can't be outsourced to a robot or reduced to an algorithm. It's about mastering the human element of the leadership function.

Imagine a simple factory with a conveyor belt. Some things go into the factory and other things come out. For example, imagine a furniture factory where lumber goes into one side, and tables come out from the other. You have input and output. Or imagine an automobile factory where steel goes in, and cars come out. Once again we have input and output. And in each case, we have a process occurring inside the factory that converts the input to the output. Pretty simple.

But now let's look at this metaphor in terms of the leader. Every morning many people walk in through the doors of your office building. They represent the raw material that you, the leader, have to work with. They are your input. And so what is the output? What are you trying to produce with these people? Results! You may be looking for financial results or competitive

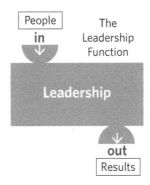

results. But whatever your goal, results are what you want. This is the leadership function: people in, results out.

Let's make a few observations. First, if something is wrong with the function, then something must be wrong with the leadership. As a leader, your job is to orchestrate the behavior of your team members in a way that produces results. The leader is the bridge between a group of acquaintances and great success.

How do you know whether or not a furniture factory is doing a good job? Simple—you look at how many quality tables they produce. It's the same with leadership. If your people aren't producing results, then something is wrong in the leadership factory. And that means you! You are the factory. The most important part of your job description is to get results from your people. So if they produce lesser results than you want, then you need to change what happens inside the factory. And that starts with you. Chances are, there is something in your attitude that is hurting the production of results.

This brings us to the second observation: the leader's job is all about people. People are your input, your raw material, and the clay from which you sculpt a masterpiece. So you can't hate any of your people. This is a problem that we sometimes observe with leaders. They have lofty dreams for success, but they are cynical and bitter about their people! This is madness! If you hate your people, then you're going to be awful at your job. Why? Because you would hate the very goose that lays your golden eggs!

This requires a shift in attitude. Start treating people as your source material—the natural element from which you construct your success.

Take as an example the Sioux people of the Great Plains. Their source material was the buffalo. They used the meat for food, the horns for tools, and the hides for shelter. They built their whole life from the buffalo, using it to survive and thrive. And accordingly, how did they treat it? They revered it! They loved it! They danced for it, ritualized it, and even made it a part of their religion. Why? Because it was the source of their success—and sustained their very lives!

Now imagine a manager at a mid-sized factory. His situation is not so different from the people in the Sioux tribe—except that his buffalo is the human being! It's the performance of human beings that can pay his bills and allow him to feed his family. It's their performance that can sustain his life. So why wouldn't he revere his people in the same way that the Sioux revered the buffaloes?

Can you imagine a winemaker who invested his life in a beautiful vineyard, but then hated grapes? It would be absurd! It's difficult even to imagine, isn't it? What's more likely? That he loves grapes! He is fascinated by them. He studies the science of grapes and even designs his own experiments in vinification. When you walk into his home, you see paintings of vineyards hanging on the walls and books about new grape varietals that he wants to cultivate. There's a passion there. A fire. Why? That's his source material! That's his fountain of life. And he reveres it.

Now, why should it be any different for a leader of people? If the winemaker hates grapes, then how skillful will he be at producing wine? Probably not very skillful at all. It works the same way in leadership. If you hate people, then you won't be very skillful at leading them. You need to love people in the same way that the Sioux love buffaloes. You need to study people and celebrate them. And this is actually more important to leadership than it is to hunting or winemaking. Because, unlike buffaloes and grapes—who are completely indifferent to adoration—people are very aware of how you feel about them. The way you treat your source material will very much impact the results you get.

And this brings us to our third and final observation: performance is the name of the game.

People produce results only when they perform. The worker has to assemble the table or construct the automobile. You can't just act on the people who walk into the factory. You need *them* to act. They can't be passive. They must be active. And the degree to which they act is of critical importance to a leader. And that's what we turn to next.

CHAPTER SUMMARY

- Individual leadership is the essence of team leadership.
- Leaders are the bridge between people and end results.
- People are your source material.
- If you dislike people, then you won't be a great leader.

ACTION ITEMS

- Identify the primary attitude you've had about people in the past (1 = you've hated people, 10 = you've absolutely loved people).

- List five scripts that will communicate your love of people (for example, "I'm constantly impressed by what people are capable of! Humans can do the most remarkable things!").

    1. _____

2. _____

_____

3. _____

_____

4. _____

_____

5. _____

_____

- List five ways to communicate your love of people nonverbally (for example, "Display a poster in your office that celebrates the heroism of humankind.").

1. _____

_____

2. _____

_____

3. _____

_____

4. _____

_____

5. _____

_____

THE EXTRA MILE

Identifying Extraordinary Performance

The second focus of this book is on extraordinary performance. People go into the leadership factory, and they produce results. They perform. They might broker sales, pour molten steel, or design marketing brochures. But they perform. That's why they're on the team. The leader's job is to elicit this performance.

Here's the major difference between leaders: some can elicit a much better performance from their team than other leaders can. And that's the difference between the good and the great. It's all about performance. Great leaders can elicit extraordinary performance from their people. And that's the focus of this book—to help you do the same.

We don't want you to inspire your people to do the bare minimum, do just enough to get by, or to sustain their mediocrity. Our focus is not on ordinary performance, but *extra*-ordinary performance. It's about pushing people to make the extra effort, run the extra mile, and go above and beyond normal expectations.

Our favorite image for this is a person who is willing to run through brick walls for his or her leader. No matter the problem, no matter the hardship. These people will give their absolute best effort. They will put it all on the line and run straight through a brick wall to achieve the team's goal.

Now it's important to realize that this level of performance is not a fantasy. It does occur, and it's realistic to pursue. For evidence of it's existence, let's turn to the customer service industry. Here extraordinary performance is easy to observe. And those in the industry know how infectious this kind of performance can be. Many companies document and circulate stories of exceptional customer service. This gives us a body of literature to examine—not as clinical experiments, but from real-world, "live combat" situations.

Let's briefly look at three classic stories from three well-known service-oriented organizations.

1) Nordstrom: At a Nordstrom store in Connecticut, a worker stumbled upon a customer's bag in the parking lot. The customer had apparently left it by accident after a shopping trip. But when the worker looked in the bag, he discovered not only her receipt, but also a full flight itinerary for a trip that she was taking that day! The Nordstrom worker guessed that she had gone directly from the store to JFK airport in New York City. So he got her phone number from the company records and called her. But she didn't pick up. He called her several more times. No luck. But the worker didn't give up. He called JFK. And after some pleading, he convinced the airport personnel to page the customer to inform her that Nordstrom still had her bags!

In this case, we see an employee going out of his way to help a customer and then running through obstacles as they came up—all just to return her bag.[10]

2) Zappos: After a woman checked into a Las Vegas hotel, she realized that she had a problem. She had forgotten to bring

her favorite pair of shoes. So she logged onto Zappos.com and looked for the shoes, hoping to find another pair. But she didn't see them on the website. And this upset her because she desperately needed those specific shoes as soon as possible. So she called the Zappos customer service line. The customer service representative searched the company database and informed her that Zappos no longer sold the shoes that she wanted. The woman was upset. But instead of letting it end there, the Zappos customer service team went to work. They located a pair of those shoes at a nearby store in Las Vegas. Then, instead of just directing the woman to the store, they sent one of their employees to buy the shoes, bring them directly to her hotel and hand deliver them to her at no extra charge.

Here again, we see a situation where a team of workers solved a problem in the face of several significant obstacles. And as to the woman who received the shoes, she learned firsthand that Zappos workers will run through brick walls to serve their customers.[11]

3) Marriott: A business traveler had checked into a Marriott hotel in Mississauga, Ontario. When he approached the front desk later that day, he said he had a big problem. He held a pair of black business slacks that belonged to his wife. He had packed her pants by mistake, and now he had no black slacks for his meeting. He had a simple request: Would they please check the lost and found for any black business slacks, or—if they found none—would they please tell him where he might buy some slacks on the way to his meeting? The Marriott workers checked the lost and found, but there wasn't anything that he could wear. Now with just ten minutes until his meeting was scheduled to start, there wasn't enough time to buy new pants. But one of the workers noticed that he happened to be the same size as the

guest. So he took off his pants, offered them to the man, and they fit! So he left for his meeting wearing the pants loaned to him by the Marriott worker. And he made it to the meeting on time.

Obviously, nobody expected the worker to take off his pants—not the guest, the employee's co-workers, or his boss. The Marriott employee would have experienced no demotions or demerits if he hadn't—giving up your own clothes just isn't something you can require of a worker. But he volunteered his pants on his own, without being asked, simply to help the guest—a stranger—get out of a jam. This is the kind of performance that goes above and beyond exceptional. And to the man who received the loan of the pants, it probably seemed like nothing could stop these Marriott workers from providing exceptional service![12]

Let's analyze what was happening in these stories. In each of these stories, there was a minimum level of service that would have been acceptable. In every case, the workers could have said, "I'm sorry—my hands are tied. This is all I can do." And that would have been acceptable. They would have been doing their jobs. But that was not what happened. They chose not to settle for acceptable performance. They went above and beyond the call of duty. They went the extra mile and found an exceptional solution. This is extraordinary performance. And although each of these examples is specifically about customer service, the scope of our discussion goes well beyond customer service. Our focus is on extraordinary performance in any field, and on working toward any goal.

Consider the 1996 Olympics, at the climax of the women's team gymnastic competition.[13] This was a moment of great anxiety for the American team as they saw their gold medal hopes come down to a single vault. But the woman standing at the beginning of the runway was seriously injured. Kerri Strug had just taken her first vault and had slipped on her landing, tearing two ligaments in her ankle. The last thing anybody with torn ankle ligaments should do is run eighty-two feet at full speed, jump as high as she can into the air, torque her body as much as possible, and then absorb all the impact of landing on her feet. Nobody would have blamed her had she decided not to take the second vault. Nobody would have held it against her. She had already done her duty. But she insisted on taking her second run. And as she ran, every step shot more and more pain up her leg. But she kept running. She took her vault and flung herself into the air...and stuck the landing! But only briefly, immediately collapsing over her ankle, unable even to get herself off the mat. But when the judges' scores flashed, she received a 9.712 (out of 10) which guaranteed the gold medal for the American team.[14] This was extraordinary performance.

Or what about the worker who stays late and works weekends so that an urgent project gets finished by the deadline? Or how about the parishioner who, upon learning that the church is unable to meet its budget, quietly and anonymously donates the money to keep it afloat? Or the daughter who holds her family together through a seemingly endless supply of patience and emotional support? Extraordinary performance can exist anywhere that people work towards a goal.

And if, as a leader, you can elicit this kind of extraordinary performance from your people, then your success will be massive. You will achieve things that now you can't even imagine.

But unfortunately, achieving massive success is not that simple. Because you won't always have a team of Olympic gold medalists to lead. And that brings us to the third and final element of this book.

CHAPTER SUMMARY

- The leader's job is to elicit excellent performance from people.
- Extraordinary performance goes above and beyond a basic job description.
- People are capable of extraordinary performance.
- You can elicit extraordinary performance through your communication and leadership styles.

ACTION ITEMS

- Identify three examples of someone on your team giving an extraordinary performance (for example, "Last quarter, Jennifer worked overtime without pay to meet the proposal deadline.").

    1. _____

    _____

    2. _____

    _____

    3. _____

    _____

- Specify three examples of the extraordinary performance you would like to see from your team today (for example, "The accountants could send personalized thank you letters to clients who pay on time.").

    1. _____

    _____

2. _____

_____

3. _____

_____

- List three ideas about how you could recognize and celebrate extraordinary performance in the the future (for example, "Write a praiseworthy article for the company's monthly newsletter.").

1. _____

_____

2. _____

_____

3. _____

_____

CHAPTER 6

LISA'S LESSON

Making the Most of Your Misfits

The third focus of this book is ordinary people. At this point, we know what we're doing (leadership) and we know what we're producing (extraordinary performance) but whom are we leading? Whom are we eliciting this extraordinary performance from? Not the exceptionally good and not the exceptionally bad. But all of those overlooked people in the middle. The average people. The ordinary.

Some books discuss how to hire and recruit the very best people—the créme de la créme. That's great, but that's not our focus. Other books discuss how to fire and discipline the very worst people. Again, that's important, but it's not our focus. We are focused on how to get extraordinary performance from

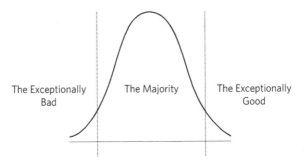

The Exceptionally Bad   The Majority   The Exceptionally Good

ordinary workers. The great people will give an extraordinary performance with or without you. The bad people will need to be reformed before they can produce at a high level—if they ever can. But average people just require leadership. These people have the potential for great performance, but they need the inspiration of a great leader to fulfill that potential. That is the subject of this book: leading average, ordinary people to greatness.

This reflects the situation of most leaders. By definition, most people are average. So it's extremely likely that your teammates are average, too, having a mixture of strengths and weaknesses. Of course, extraordinary people do exist. And some leaders have the ability to buy and recruit anybody that they want. But most of us do not have that ability. Most of us are more like Teddy Roosevelt and Sir Francis Drake—leaders who don't have the luxury of the first pick. Most leaders aren't given a team of seasoned achievers. Most people simply have to do the best they can, with what they have, where they are.

That's the bad news. But here's the good news: ordinary people can do remarkable things! They can step up and give an exceptional performance. And when they perform, they can help you beat even the fiercest competition.

Here's one of our favorite examples. The most dominant team in professional baseball is the New York Yankees. They have won more World Series titles than any other team, by nearly 300 percent (Yankees 27, Cardinals 11)! And in the 2003 season, it seemed they were all but guaranteed to win one more, and add another notch to their championship belt. But the Florida Marlins, the upstart team that was up against the Yankees, wouldn't give up so easily.[15]

On paper, the Yankees were set to win the series. Their payroll was three times larger ($164 million versus $54 million), and they had won more games in the regular season than the Marlins had. They had a team of all-star veterans, while the Marlins fielded a team of young, untested players who had often been overlooked. And if that weren't enough, due to a recent rule change, New York was awarded home-field advantage. So if you were betting who would win, it would have been smart to pick the Yankees. And many people did—the Yankees were heavily favored.

But the numbers can't predict performance. And during that series, the Marlins found a way to keep fighting. The critical moment came in game four of the seven-game series. The Yankees were up two games to one. If they won game four, then the series would be all but over. So this game was crucial. And although the Marlins had seized an early lead, the Yankees had closed the gap and pushed the game into extra innings. No runs in the 10th... no runs in the 11th... the tension was mounting.

Then, in the 12th inning, a player named Alex González stepped to the plate. Who was Alex González? Let's first acknowledge that anyone who makes it to the major leagues is incredibly talented, and that making the majors is a huge achievement in and of itself. That said, on that grand stage in 2003, Alex González was not a superstar. He would be considered an ordinary player by World Series Standards. He had made the All-Star game four years earlier. But in 2001 he led all of Major League Baseball in errors committed by a shortstop. His batting average in 2003 had been .256. Not terrible, but not great either. It was ordinary. Worse yet, he was in a bit of a slump, going only 1 for 13 so far in the World Series. People didn't expect much from him. He was just ordinary.

But whether Alex González was ordinary or not, this was his moment. He stepped to the plate at the bottom of the 12th inning and gave the performance of a lifetime, hitting a walk-off home run to win the game for the Marlins. This tied the series and gave the Marlins the momentum to win the championship two games later.

Now, here's a question, how does an underdog like the Florida Marlins defeat a juggernaut like the New York Yankees? And here's the answer: you need guys like Alex González to hit home runs when it counts. That's how you win. That's how an upstart emerges as the victor. You don't need to outspend them on talent—that's probably impossible, anyway. You just need your ordinary players to give an extraordinary performance in the critical moments.

The same is as true for you as it was for the Marlins. If you get your ordinary people to hit home runs at the critical moments, then you can out-compete anyone. Extraordinary performance from ordinary people beats mediocre performance from exceptional people every time. And this is something that you can bring about. This is the leadership push.

But if you don't believe this, then your motivational efforts will backfire.

A good example of this is Lisa.[16] Lisa was the manager of a single location for an international, health-care company chain. And we were called in because her location was in turmoil. Bickering and infighting abounded on her team. They couldn't seem to complete their critical tasks—and as a result, customer service suffered. Worst of all, revenues had been steadily declining.

When we distributed anonymous surveys, employees said that they "hated coming into work" and that they thought the location was "a lost cause." In short, Lisa was not accomplishing her goals. Her people were not performing under her leadership. The location was failing and her job was at risk.

When we met with Lisa and asked her why her location was so troubled, she had a long list of reasons. But, like many struggling leaders, her primary scapegoat was her team. For hours, she told us all about their poor performance and how they stubbornly resisted her productivity-boosting efforts. She listed their weaknesses, and all of their past mistakes. She clearly felt that they were the reason for the location's failure.

Interesting.

After meeting with several of Lisa's key people, the true reasons for the problems at the location became clear: the cause was Lisa herself! She yelled at the members of her team. She was harsh with them. She pointed out their faults. She always saw the worst in them. Her whole pattern of personal interaction was unpleasant. This caused her people to shut down and drag their feet. And it created a culture of blame that wrecked havoc with the team.

To be fair, Lisa was a smart, professional woman. And she had a very kind heart when she didn't feel threatened. That made it all the more surprising that she had such a bad relationship with her people. It was as if she became a different person when she stepped into her leadership role. What was happening?

Lisa was hardworking. And so she naturally expected the members of her team to have the same standards as she did. But they didn't. So when they gave an average performance, Lisa lost her cool. She scolded them and treated them as if they were awful people. But they weren't awful people. They were ordinary. Remember, exceptionally good people can give an extraordinary performance all on their own, but ordinary people need a good leader to elicit the extraordinary. And that's okay. That's just how the world works.

But Lisa didn't understand that. She didn't allow for that. She wanted her team to be exceptionally good people. And when they weren't, she treated them harshly.

Think about the effect of that kind of harsh treatment. It's like noticing that a peach tree doesn't have any peaches. And then trying to elicit peaches by withholding the very things the tree needs—such as sunlight, soil, and water! What would happen if you treated a tree that way? It would wither and die. And that was exactly what was happening to Lisa's team! Her actions weren't eliciting extraordinary performance. Instead, they were causing poor performance! Her team was suffering, because she didn't understand how to lead them.

So we put her into a monthly coaching program. And once she became aware of the problem, everything at the company began to change. She realized that the largest obstacle to her goals was her own behavior. She realized that she could have the greatest strategies in the world, but it wouldn't matter if she couldn't get her people to perform. Until she did, she would not be able to achieve success.

During her coaching, it was as if a light went off in her mind. She adopted a gardener's attitude, and stopped trying to elicit excellent performance through intimidation. Instead, she started thinking about how to help her people grow. She started valuing them and inspiring them in a positive way that they responded to. Within just a few months, she completely transformed her leadership style.

The result was nothing short of a miracle. Morale improved and the pace of work at the office quickened. There was a decrease in the number of employee conflicts. Interoffice cliques began to disband. But best of all was that her numbers started to increase. The company's customer service scores went up by

31 percent, communication scores jumped by 45 percent, and teamwork scores increased by 34 percent. And best of all, revenue began to climb. This was the success that Lisa so desperately wanted from the beginning. And she achieved it over just a few months—all because of a shift in her leadership.

Now, to be honest, we had met all of her workers. And well... They didn't exactly look like a group of winners. It was apparent that many didn't make personal hygiene a high priority. A few clearly did not take care of their health. And some had a facial expression that must have developed through years of cynicism. In truth, they really didn't look like a group of winners. They looked like a group of misfits. And you could see why Lisa might blame them for the poor results.

The first big task was for Lisa to change her attitude. Then, she needed to look at her team and tell herself with a straight face, "Sic Parvis Magna." Greatness comes from small beginnings. And she needed to honestly believe that. She needed to stop taking their poor performance personally. Instead, she needed to treat that behavior as weeds in a garden, and calmly address it. And she had to make the personal decision to build them up rather than tear them down, finding potential where it had been previously overlooked.

And she did! She learned to love her group of average workers. They were her source material, her buffaloes! She was never going to lead a group of Olympians, so she learned to love the misfits instead. The underdogs. Her ragtag team. And this brought a dramatic change in her results.

But that change in attitude was only the first step. It was necessary, but it wasn't enough for Lisa just to start thinking differently. She also needed to start *acting* differently. First, she needed to believe that the leadership push was possible. Then, she needed to execute it. So we introduced her to new skills and helped her practice them during our coaching meetings. This is what catalyzed the tremendous change in her. And the skills we taught Lisa are the skills we are going to explore for the remainder of this book.

CHAPTER SUMMARY

- Most of your workers are ordinary, and that's okay.
- Ordinary people can perform at extraordinary levels.
- Ordinary people won't give an extraordinary performance without good leadership.
- You can beat the juggernauts—you just need your ordinary people to hit home runs at the crucial time.
- For ordinary people to perform differently, the leader must make proactive changes.

ACTION ITEMS

- List five of your teammates and list three strengths for each person. Then identify a large goal that each teammate could help you achieve if they used their strengths to give an extraordinary performance.

Name	Strengths	Big Goal
Example: Molly Jefferson	Persuasive Friendly Ambitious	She could close a deal with the largest customer in the region

1. _____

_____

_____

Name	Strengths	Big Goal

2. _____

3. _____

4. _____

5. _____

PART II

THE KÖHLER EFFECT

CHAPTER 7

HOLDING THE HAMMER

Engaging Your Workers through Delegation

I f you were to choose the most successful nonprofit of all time, you would have several very good options. You might choose the Red Cross, a humanitarian aid organization that has provided disaster relief for over 100 years. Or you might choose Doctors Without Borders, who sends medical professionals into war-torn and disease-stricken regions. Beyond these two, there are many more excellent nonprofit organizations that have accomplished remarkable things.

But if you were going to make a list of the most effective nonprofits, you would probably have to include Habitat for Humanity.[17]

Founded in 1976, Habitat for Humanity is a much younger organization than the venerable old Red Cross. But Habitat for Humanity quickly established an oversize influence in the communities it served. Their vision is that everyone should have a decent place to live. But in the world we live in, many in poverty can't afford to pay rent—much less to buy their own home. Habitat for Humanity helps to bridge this gap. And they have an unusual way of doing it—through volunteer labor.

Habitat for Humanity coordinates and manages the volunteer construction of high-quality homes for qualified families. They reach out to the community and ask for volunteers. And when people offer to help, new houses are built. This doesn't just transform the lives of the new homeowners, but it also catalyzes change in the community—creating unlikely friendships, transforming neighborhoods and revitalizing cities.

Habitat for Humanity has been remarkably successful with this businesses model. They've grown from a being a small, regional charity to an international organization, with offices in South Africa, Thailand, Slovakia, and Costa Rica. They recruit over 2.1 million volunteers annually and, in 2013, they celebrated the completion of their 800,000th home.[18] Today, they build and renovate homes around the world, providing an opportunity for millions of people to lend a hand in helping their disadvantaged neighbors.

How can one account for this huge success? How does such an unlikely strategy produce such extraordinary results? After all, the success of their business model depends on volunteer work. And it's not easy work. A long day at a worksite can leave you exhausted and sore. Don't most people hate hard work? And workdays are typically on the weekend. Don't you usually have to pay someone overtime to work on Saturday or Sunday? All it would take is for the volunteers to decide to stay home, and the whole organization would collapse. How in the world do you prevent that from happening on a single, beautiful sunny day, much less every year since 1976?

The answer is a leadership secret that's hiding in plain sight.

To understand this secret, let's take a peek behind the curtain of Habitat for Humanity's leadership. But not the executive leadership at the corporate offices. Let's look at the volunteer leadership, out on the worksites.[19]

Here's the typical structure for a day at the worksite. Volunteers show up, either in groups or as individuals, and check in with a coordinator. After being assigned a task, they meet with their foreman and join a crew. Depending on the stage of the projects and the number of houses under construction at any one time, there may be anywhere from one to several crews. Volunteers work, break for lunch, and then work again until late afternoon.

The critical component of this model—the driving force that makes it possible—is the foremen. They direct and supervise the volunteer workers. They maintain the precarious balance between safety and progress, managing the often-inexperienced volunteers and assigning jobs that they can safely handle. The foremen keep the worksite from slipping into chaos and make it resemble, as much as possible, the worksite of a traditional construction project.

How does one become a foreman? Typically, they have construction experience, either privately or through volunteering for Habitat for Humanity in the past. And they have to show a basic level of interest and competence. Then they attend a leadership-training program, which typically lasts a full weekend. In this program, they review the basics of construction and safety, along with instruction on how to handle the frequent problems that foremen face on the worksite. And at some point during the weekend, they are given the secret of Habitat for Humanity's success—the rule that you *must* follow to be a successful foreman.

Don't hold the hammer.

What? How do you build a house without holding a hammer? You don't. And that's the point. It's not about *you* building the house and feeling like a hero. It's about the *volunteers* building the house and feeling like heroes. The foremen's job is not to build a house, but to build *heroes*. And that means that the only time you hold a hammer is when you put it into the volunteer's hand.

Here's how this principal works: on build day, the foreman's job is to put volunteers to work. But if you are the foreman and you hold a hammer (or any tool) in your hand, then you are liable to use it. We all have an instinct to solve a problem when we hold the solution. And if you're walking around with a hammer, it's very tempting to start swinging at a few nails. But if a foreman hammers in a nail, that means that a volunteer isn't hammering that nail. The volunteer is most likely just watching from the sidelines.

Now, what does that matter? After all, the foreman is probably more skilled than the volunteer. He can drive the nail faster, straighter, and with less risk of injury. At first glance, you might think that *only* a foreman should hold the hammer. And it would seem ridiculous to ban such an experienced builder from holding it. After all, they are the experts! And the whole point is to build a house, right?

Almost. The point is actually to build a *lot* of houses. And to build a lot of houses, you need a lot of volunteers. Not just to swing hammers, but also to donate money, donate supplies, and work behind the scene. And if you want to build a lot of houses, then you need to understand what motivates those volunteers.

When volunteers show up in the morning to a worksite, they want to work. They already feel inspired by Habitat for Humanity's lofty vision, and they want to help. They want to contribute. They want something to do. That's how they are going to feel good about themselves. They want to work on something meaningful. They want to take photos and post them on social media. They want to brag to their friends about their sore muscles and show them their blisters. They want the self-esteem that only comes from a long day of hard work on a meaningful task. This is why they show up.

But what if things don't go as planned? Imagine that a volunteer, full of optimism, shows up on Saturday morning to a smoothly running operation. The foremen are holding the hammers and doing most of the work. The volunteer crews just stand and watch, only occasionally being asked to fetch a tool or throw out some garbage. As the day moves on, the volunteers get competitive for each job that the foremen toss their way. Some volunteers take the initiative and busy themselves with a task, like pushing a broom or cleaning some tools. Others just disengage, sitting in the corner and fiddling with their phones.

The job gets done, but at what cost? How many of those volunteers are going to feel proud of their work? How many are going to be glad that they spent their Saturday volunteering? How many are going to brag about their experience positively to their friends? How many of them will donate in the future? And—perhaps most importantly—how many will ever come back?

When the foremen hold the hammers, they take the experience away from the volunteers, who came to work, not to watch someone else work. So the foreman must put the hammer into the volunteers' hands. The foreman needs to give them an important job. Something meaningful. Not busy work, but the most important thing that their level of competence allows.

This is the secret to Habitat for Humanity's success. The foremen put the volunteers to work, not primarily for the completion of the house, but for the pleasure that working hard for a good cause provides. They deliberately slow progress on a project to give volunteers a meaningful experience.

What does this accomplish?

First, the volunteers spread the word. They are going to publicize how great the workday was. They are going to blast it on social media, write about it on Christmas cards, and talk about it at cocktail parties. More people are going to hear about Habitat for Humanity. And people are going to see how happy it makes other people to volunteer. This will naturally bring in more support and volunteers. This word-of-mouth advertising is precious and can bring a massive flood of support and resources into the organization

Second, the volunteers will come back. If they have a great experience, then they are going to want to do it again—three, four, or maybe five times a year. They might even become lifetime volunteers, working both on site and behind the scenes. Think about dating—first impressions can last a lifetime. And if you enjoyed your first date, then you are probably going to want to go on another one. And dating can eventually turn into marriage. Not always. But if you want to get married, a good date is a good start!

Third, you learn about the volunteers. You can't assess a person's skill set while they are sitting on the bench. You need to watch them swing a hammer to see how well they do it. And if you don't, you're likely to overlook valuable people. Imagine that a man from a local construction company comes in. He's highly skilled. He's in a position to donate lots of resources to Habitat for Humanity's cause. But if he's told to push a broom in an empty room, then nobody is going to recognize what he can do. And he's going to watch foremen do tasks that he knows he could do better. He's going to disengage, never to return. The foremen would have done a better job of leadership by identifying him and putting him to work on something that requires great skill.

Fourth, the experience builds the skill set of the volunteers. Not everyone is going to be highly skilled when they show up. And here's the secret. If they never swing the hammer, they are never going to get any better! If you make them watch from the sidelines, they are never going to do anything other than watch. But if you give them the hammer, and they keep coming back, then eventually you will have a highly skilled worker.

Finally, participation encourages greater commitment. If volunteers have a fantastic workday experience, they often turn into donors who deliver major support outside the construction site. Imagine a wealthy woman who is shopping for a charity to benefit from her philanthropy. So she volunteers, incognito, at a Habitat for Humanity's work site. What if she spends all day standing around and pushing a broom in an empty room? Then she will be on to considering the next charity, and Habitat for Humanity will have missed a big opportunity. But what if she swings a hammer and plays an important role in the construction? Then she's going to have a great time. And she's going to write that big check when she gets home. This kind of thing happens. And Habitat for Humanity's leaders make it happen.

All of this is accomplished by one simple rule for leaders: Don't hold the hammer. Don't do a task that a volunteer can do. And if you can find a volunteer for every job, then sit back and watch. Don't hold the hammer. This rule has allowed Habitat for Humanity to change the lives of millions of people.

The success of Habitat for Humanity teaches us a crucial lesson. People want work that matters. They want to feel that they are making a valuable contribution. And they won't feel that unless you give them an important job. They look to leaders to connect them with something serious and meaningful. Just think about all of the motivated volunteers who show up to a Habitat for Humanity worksite with no idea what they are going to do. That was the brilliant insight of Habitat for Humanity: there are plenty of people willing to help if only someone can figure out how to use them. They are ready to work. They just need a hammer.

Delegation is a tool of abundance. It increases the level of work, the level of competence, and the strategic efficacy of the organization. And for these reasons alone, it's a foundational tool of leadership—something that every leader must master. But it also motivates individual performance. That's our focus in this book. Delegation is an essential element of the leadership push. And we want you to understand why it would make a person work harder. Furthermore, we want to show you how to harness this power for the success of your team, and of your own leadership.

As we will see in the next chapter, the secret lies in the motivational impact of a team.

CHAPTER SUMMARY

- Money is not the only motivator, or even the best one.
- People want meaningful work.
- It's motivational to give people an important job to do.
- Delegation is a tool of abundance.

ACTION ITEMS

- List three times that you've witnessed people get motivated after being given an important task (for example, "When my son was finally old enough to mow the lawn, he felt important—and mowed it better than I did!").

  1. _____

  _____

  2. _____

  _____

  3. _____

  _____

- List five important tasks that you could delegate to members of your team (for example, "securing vendors for the building project").

  1. _____

  _____

  2. _____

  _____

  3. _____

  _____

  4. _____

  _____

  5. _____

  _____

CHAPTER 8

SHARED BARBELLS

Motivating Workers through Teamwork

A team is a group of people who work together to achieve a common goal. And teams have some unique motivational properties. Simply put, people work harder to prevent letting their teammates down. So when people feel like an important part of a team, they will give a greater effort than when they work by themselves.

This was first identified in the 1920s by the German psychologist Otto Köhler. And it has since become known as the Köhler effect.[20]

Köhler's study was simple. He had members of the Berlin Rowing Club barbell curl a heavy barbell (44 kg, or about 97 lbs.). As the control, he recorded everybody's maximum number of repetitions while curling the barbell solo. This gave him the base strength and level of endurance of each athlete. Then he put people into groups and had them curl the barbell all together, increasing the weight proportionately. For example, when he put three people on a single barbell, he tripled the weight (from 44 kg to 132 kgs). Notice that this made the participants dependent on each other for performance. If one person gave out, then the other two could not continue—at least not for very long. One person could not quit without letting the other two down. So each person had an immediate social motivation to keep curling.

So what happened? Köhler found that groups completed more repetitions than the weakest members were able to lift on their own. In other words, the weaker members performed at a higher level when put in a situation where others depended on them. There were no financial incentives involved—just social expectations and the unwillingness to look bad in front of their peers.

And we have since learned that this doesn't just apply to physical tasks. Subsequent studies have not only replicated Köhler's original result, but they have also shown that the Köhler effect works for computational and visually oriented tasks as well.[21] They all show the same thing: people work harder to avoid letting their peers down.

In another study, researchers tested how long people were willing to ride a fitness bike.[22] In the first group, each participant rode the bike alone in the lab, and the researchers timed how long they rode. This was the control. In the second group, participants rode with virtual partners, whom the researchers projected onto a nearby screen. This may seem like nothing since the partner was not real, but this simple act caused their time to double compared to the isolated group. That's a huge gain. But then there was a third group. This time, researchers told the participants that they were on a *team* and that their score would contribute to a *team score*. This tripled the time that each participant persisted on their bikes!

Think about that: the simple act of telling people that their actions contributed to a team score tripled their productivity. So if they would otherwise ride their bike for an hour, now they would ride it for three hours. That's an incredible motivational gain. And that's what happens when the Köhler effect comes into play. People work harder when their performance matters to their team.

One of the most interesting real-world illustrations comes from the Olympic games. Now, if ever the Köhler effect should not apply, you would think it would be at the Olympics. People who make the Olympics are highly trained athletes. They have trained diligently for years to reach the top of their sport. They have devoted their lives to a single goal—to medal at the games. Few people ever display the level of dedication as Olympic athletes. Surely, these people wouldn't be affected by intersocial motivation. Surely, if there were an exception to the Köhler effect, we would find it at the Olympic games. Right?

Researchers began by analyzing the performance of swimmers at the 2008 Olympic games.[23] Why swimming? Because it's the perfect laboratory to test the Köhler effect. Athletes compete both individually and in relays, where four swimmers combine their performances for an overall time. This allowed the researchers to compare the split times of swimmers when they were competing only for themselves to their times when other athletes depended on them directly. Olympic athletes have every reason to perform their hardest in each event, and judges measure results with excruciating accuracy. It's the perfect research laboratory.

What did the researchers find? Did the Köhler effect hold up?

After analyzing the data, they found that swimmers posted faster times in the freestyle relay than in the individual races. But this was true only for people in the later relay positions. In other words, if you were a freestyle swimmer at the third or fourth leg of a relay race, then your split would be faster than when you swam that same distance in an individual race. The athletes were the same, the water was the same, the cameras that recorded their split-second finishes were the same, but the intersocial dependency was different. And that led to a better performance. The Köhler effect holds.

Here is a classic example.[24] The superstar of the 2008 Beijing games was Michael Phelps. He was on a quest to break the record for winning the most gold medals at any single games. At the time, the record was seven. He needed eight. But Phelps was up to the challenge, winning a gold medal in each of his five individual races. The world was in awe of his talent. But he couldn't break the record on his own. To win eight gold medals, he also needed to win in the relay races. That meant he had to depend on his teammates. If they failed to perform, then this record-breaking moment would pass him by.

The critical moment came in the 100 m freestyle relay. The United States had not won this race in twelve years. And this year, the French were heavily favored. Even the American commentators admitted that there was almost no way for the USA to win. The French were too good. But everyone knew that this was a do-or-die moment for Phelps. If the American team couldn't win gold at this event, then his hopes would be dashed.

Phelps opened the race and established a lead over the French, which continued throughout the second leg. But as the third leg unfolded, the Americans began to fall behind. France took a commanding lead. The American who dove into the pool for the final leg was Jason Lezak. And he was a full body length behind first place, chasing the Frenchman who at the time held the world record in that event. The world held its breath.

What followed was the greatest performance in Olympic swimming history. When Lezak started swimming, the announcers said that second place was his only hope. But after the final turn, Lezak seemed to gain ground. It was slow at first, but then it was undeniable. But there wasn't much time! Lezak kept pushing and kept gaining ground. The crowd couldn't believe it! They were neck and neck in the homestretch! At the final push, Lezak threw his arm forward toward the finish... and won! He edged out the Frenchman by only 0.08 seconds—the narrowest margin in the event's history!

This dramatic, come-from-behind victory won the USA the gold medal. And Michael Phelps would go on to win eight gold medals. It was a total success—a highpoint in American Olympic history.

And it also illustrates the Köhler effect.

In the 100 m freestyle, Lezak was in the fourth position. This qualifies him for the Köhler effect. And elsewhere in the games, Lezak swam the same event as an individual, giving us a comparison race. So how did his times compare? When Lezak swam individually, he posted a time of 47.67 seconds. But when Lezak swam during the relay, he posted a time of 46.06 seconds—fully 1.61 seconds faster!

If Lezak had posted a time of 47.67 during the relay, then the Americans would have lost. It's that simple. He needed the motivation of his team to elicit his record-breaking performance. The Köhler effect won the American team gold.

But maybe this was a fluke. Maybe there was some anomaly about the 2008 games that produced the illusion of the Köhler effect. So in 2012, researchers did a follow-up study where they crunched data from the previous four Olympic games.[25] Again, they found that athletes swam faster in later positions of relay races than they did in the individual version of the same race. Consider what that means. The data from four Olympic games included different generations of athletes. And it included athletes from all over the world. It's not a clinical trial on a college campus performed with volunteer undergraduates. It's with people competing at the top level, who have given their lives for this single event that occurs only once every four years. And yet, remarkably, the Köhler effect held.

What was happening here? The researchers called this outcome, "motivation gains due to social indispensability." When people need you—that is, when your performance is indispensable to your group's success—then you work harder. And the more people count on you, the more you feel important to the cause—and then the more likely you are to rise to the occasion.

We see this when athletes lift barbells in groups. Each person is indispensable to the team's overall performance. If one person fails, then the whole team fails. That's social indispensability. We also see this approximated in the bike study. When people find out that their score will contribute to a group score, they feel like the team, whoever they were, depend on their performance. That's social indispensability. So their performance increases. And in the swimming relays, a single person's poor performance can prevent their teammates from realizing their dreams of Olympic gold, something that they have dreamed about since childhood. And it can all be shattered if a swimmer gives a poor performance. That's social indispensability. That's the Köhler effect. And it leads to big motivational gains.

Here's the rule with the Köhler effect: the more socially indispensable a person feels, the more effort that person will make.

For example, an ordinary saleswoman might make 100 cold calls on her own. But if her sales figures contribute to a team score, then she might make 120. If pushing that sales number up will mean that her coworker can pay his daughter's medical bills, then she might make 150. And if she knows that the whole branch will close and everyone will lose their jobs unless she can double her productivity, then she might make 200 cold calls. As her feelings of social indispensability increase, so does her performance. That's the Köhler effect.

The Köhler Effect

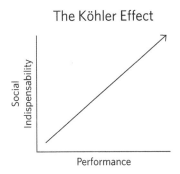

The Köhler effect seems to suggest that people work harder for others than they do for themselves. This claim is not intended to deny that people often work incredibly hard in isolation. However, the Köhler effect says that social indispensability provides a powerful, concrete form of motivation. And when all other things are equal, social indispensability increases performance.

Let's also notice something else. The Köhler effect is primarily unconscious. Olympic swimmers don't start a relay race with the thought, "Now that people depend on me, I'm going to swim harder than I did on my individual race." They think nothing of the sort. They begin each race with the thought, "I'm going to swim as fast as I possibly can." And yet they nevertheless swim faster for the relay.

Now, for the sake of accuracy, let's recognize a few limitations. These are caveats that appeared in the research. They are conditions where the Köhler effect might be expected to activate, but doesn't. And we should acknowledge them.

First, back in 1920 during the original testing, Köhler himself found that the motivational gains disappeared when the strength of the participants were greatly mismatched. For example, when he paired a weak lifter with two very strong lifters, the discrepancy seemed to demotivate the weaker lifter. Mismatched individuals would give up before they even started, negating the motivational gains. However, keep in mind that this occurred in the clinical environment, where people probably didn't feel that their performance was relatively as important to their peers as, say, during the Olympics. But it's something that appeared in the research, and we should mention it.

Second, the Köhler effect goes away when it's difficult to assess another's relative performance relative to your own. The researchers discovered this when analyzing the four years of Olympic swimming data. They found that the Köhler effect applied to swimmers in freestyle relays, where everyone was swimming with the same stroke. But the gains disappeared during the medley relays, where each swimmer used a different stroke (butterfly, backstroke, breaststroke, or freestyle). The researchers suggested this occurred because the swimmers couldn't know how well everybody else was doing in real time. Individual swimmers could, in a sense, hide their performance from the group by hiding behind the "apples to oranges" comparisons between strokes. They lost the immediate, easy-to-compare pressure. And so the Köhler effect failed.

With these caveats, we see that it's not just social indispensability that matters. It's social indispensability with reasonable accountability. And for this, we can compare the failed versions of both the mismatched lifters and the medley swimmers.

The medley swimmers were composed of Olympic-caliber athletes, so the swimmers could reasonably expect their relay team members to perform at a high level. But when the relay required different strokes—strokes that not all of the team members had equal experience with—the level of immediate, concrete accountability dropped. So the Köhler effect failed.

We get the opposite problem in the weight-lifting example. When three people hold a barbell and curl it together, there is immediate feedback on performance. You know exactly which people are pulling their weight and which are not. If someone quits, then it's immediately obvious to everyone else who did. But when the strength levels are grossly mismatched, then the lifters don't have a reasonable expectation of performance. So they give up before they even begin. Again, the Köhler effect fails.

You need immediate, concrete pressure to activate the Köhler effect. There can be no room for hiding. There can be no room for excuses. There can be no time for reflection or analysis. Either the Köhler effect happens immediately, during the moment, or it doesn't. Without reasonable accountability, the feelings of social indispensability will not arise.

However, even in the face of these caveats, we need to recognize the potential power of the Köhler effect. When you meet its conditions, it unleashes motivation and brings out a higher level of performance. And when you tap into its power, then you will powerfully engage your people. You will experience for yourself that social indispensability causes ordinary people to work harder for their peers than they do for themselves.

This is the source of the leadership push that answers the problem of motivation. How do you inspire ordinary people to give an extraordinary effort? You trigger the Köhler effect.

You give them a hammer and make them feel like an important member of the team. You make them feel their own social indispensability.

CHAPTER SUMMARY

- People work harder when they feel like important members of a team.
- The team dynamic gives meaning and importance to a task.
- The Köhler effect: a worker's performance rises alongside social indispensability.
- The Köhler effect doesn't activate without reasonable accountability.

ACTION ITEMS

- Estimate your team's current feelings of social indispensability on the team (1 = there are no feelings of social indispensability, 10 = workers feel that they are desperately dependent on each other).

- List five ways that members of your team depend on each other (for example, "When the salespeople give presentations, they depend on the marketing team producing brochures without errors.").

  1. _____

2. _____

_____

3. _____

_____

4. _____

_____

5. _____

_____

- Brainstorm five ways to show people their social indispensability (for example, "Show marketing workers the footage
  of salespeople presenting their brochures to prospects.").

1. _____

_____

2. _____

_____

3. _____

_____

4. _____

_____

5. _____

_____

CHAPTER 9

KÖHLER'S CONE

Establishing Social Indispensability

T he Köhler effect operates by social indispensability. So to maximize your ability to motivate with the Köhler effect, you need to understand how that works.

First, let's establish a clear definition of the word "indispensable." To be indispensable means that you are absolutely necessary. The operation cannot go forward without you. Being indispensable is more than just being important—something can be important without being indispensable. For example, money is important to your life. Almost everything you want in some way requires, or is affected by, money. So it's very important. But oxygen is indispensable. You can imagine ways to get by without money, but you can't live without oxygen. If you don't get oxygen, then no other parts of your life will work. Oxygen is indispensable to living. Important people are important, but when you're indispensable, nothing works without you.

But indispensability alone isn't enough. You need *social* indispensability. This means that you aren't just absolutely necessary to *any* project, you're indispensable to a project where other people depend on you—you are indispensable to a team. And if you don't do your job, then this team will suffer.

The project depends on you, and your teammates depend on the project. So other people are counting on you. That's social indispensability.

To unlock the benefits of the Köhler effect, you need to establish both elements of social indispensability: the indispensability of the task and the social dependency with one's peers. Although these forces are interrelated, let's first look at them individually.

We will represent these two elements spatially, using a triangle and a circle.

The Task Triangle represents the indispensability of the actual task. As you move up the triangle, you find jobs that are increasingly necessary. As you move down, the jobs get more superfluous. At the very bottom are the jobs that don't help the project at all. There are many of these tasks. For example, watching a baseball game isn't going to help you build a house. It doesn't help your progression one way or another. It may help with something else—such as helping you to relax at the end of the day—but it's completely unnecessary to the construction of the home. As far as your building project is concerned, it has little or no value. It's extraneous.

The Task Triangle

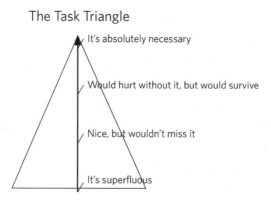

It's absolutely necessary

Would hurt without it, but would survive

Nice, but wouldn't miss it

It's superfluous

At the very top, you find the tasks which are indispensable. These are the critical tasks that the project simply cannot succeed without. Regarding home construction, your walls are indispensable. You can have an interesting space without walls—maybe a breezeway or a patio—but not a whole house. A house needs walls, so walls are indispensable. These tasks at the top are the kind that make people feel indispensable.

This brings us to the social element—the Social Circle.

This circle represents the team element, reflecting the extent to which people feel like they are part of a social group. Outside of the circle are the people who are definitely not on the team. They have no camaraderie with the members of the team—they might even be enemies! In either case, the Köhler effect doesn't activate outside of the circle.

The Social Circle

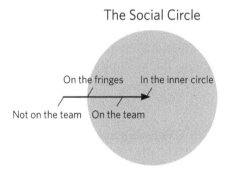

But things begin to change as you move towards the center of the circle. Once you cross the threshold, you start to feel like a member of the team. Your sense of camaraderie isn't very high yet, but it is building. And if there is ever a crisis that requires the team to pull together, then you would be counted and included.

Think of it like travelers on the Oregon Trail who circled their wagons. When pioneers felt threatened, either by marauders or by dangerous animals, they would stop moving forward in a single file. Instead, they would arrange their wagons in a protective circle, so that no single wagon would be more exposed than any other. At this moment, you knew whether or not you were on the team. If you were in the circle, then you were a member of the team. If you weren't, then you were considered a stranger. You are either "one of us" or "one of them" depending on whether or not you are in the social circle.

At the center is what you might call the inner circle. This is where camaraderie is the highest. People here feel closely connected to the team. They feel like true family. And they feel comfortable in the knowledge that they are in the inner sanctum. They are confident with their social inclusion. They don't ever feel that their position on the team is threatened. They are one of the insiders.

Now let's bring these two shapes together. What happens when you combine a triangle with a circle? You get a cone. In our case, we combine the Social Circle with the Task Triangle.

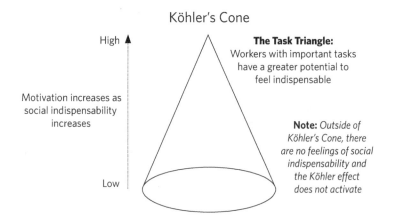

Köhler's Cone

High ▲

Motivation increases as
social indispensability
increases

Low

The Task Triangle:
Workers with important tasks
have a greater potential to
feel indispensable

Note: *Outside of
Köhler's Cone, there
are no feelings of social
indispensability and
the Köhler effect
does not activate*

The Social Circle:
Workers with strong social intimacy have
a greater potential to feel indispensable

These two elements combine to activate social indispensability. We call this Köhler's Cone.

Köhler's Cone represents a worker's feeling of social indispensability. The Task Triangle and Social Circle interact to compound the motivational effect that either could produce alone. The potential for social indispensability is higher when workers feel themselves to be in the center of the circle. Likewise, the potential for social indispensability is highest when workers feel their task to be of maximal importance. Together, the potential for social indispensability is greatest where the triangle is highest and the circle is at its center.

Think of the volume of the cone as the number of people who can do a task. At the bottom of the cone, at the level of low task necessity, anyone can do the job. Why? Because it doesn't matter if it gets done or not. So performance isn't a factor. You could give the job to a monkey and it wouldn't matter. The volume of people who can do it is enormous.

Here's how Köhler's Cone works, the strength of the Köhler effect increases as you move up the cone. The further up the cone you get, the fewer people there are who can replace you, both in the task and the social intimacy. So your job becomes ever more indispensable. People need you, and no one can replace you—which makes you want to work harder. That's the Köhler effect in action.

Notice that both the circle and the triangle are necessary, providing different motivational benefits. One has curves like a hug. The other has straight lines like a ladder. The circle provides social pressure. The triangle provides task pressure. Too much circle and no triangle, and people suffocate beneath the weight of the team. Too much triangle and no circle, and they leave the team altogether. But together, they generate strong motivation.

Remember that Köhler's Cone represents the feelings of social indispensability that exist in an individual worker. Each worker can draw different conclusions about his or her level of importance and social intimacy. This means that several positions of the cone are possible.

Köhler's Cone

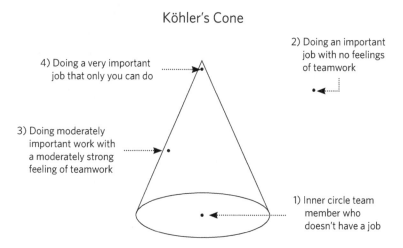

4) Doing a very important job that only you can do

2) Doing an important job with no feelings of teamwork

3) Doing moderately important work with a moderately strong feeling of teamwork

1) Inner circle team member who doesn't have a job

Position 1 is at the base of the cone and in the very center. This represents a teammate from the inner circle who either lacks a task or has a task that isn't very important. In this position, the Köhler effect doesn't activate. People in this position need a more important task. They need to be engaged through better delegation. When most of your people are in this position, your team has a "country club" culture. People feel included, but nothing important is getting done.

Here's an example of a worker in Position 1. A sibling co-inherits a business with his sister. This man sits on the executive board and attends the most senior of meetings. But he doesn't have a real role in the company. His sister is the CEO and she makes all of the decisions without him. He merely shows up for ceremonial proceedings. And yet, he is one of the few people who can reach his sister for a private audience. He is at the ground floor of Köhler's Cone—central to the circle, but on the bottom of the triangle.

Position 2 is at a high level, but is outside of the Social Circle. This represents isolated workers who perform an important task. They have no feelings of teamwork relative to their task. So they're completely outside of the cone and receive no benefit from the Köhler effect. Such workers need to form bonds with their teammates. They need to be engaged through better team building. When most of your people are in this position, your team has a "survivalist" culture. People perform relatively important work, but they feel alone, and they must fight for survival against rival workers.

For an example, consider a traveling salesperson. He closes the big deals which keep his team afloat. But while his teammates work together all day in the office, he is on the road. He doesn't know them very well—only hearing from them when he's made a mistake. He spends more time alone in roadside diners than with his teammates. So when a competitor offers him a more stable job opportunity, he feels no loyalty to his teammates back at the office. He knows that he's important to them, but he doesn't really care. They are nice people, but they just don't feel like his team. They don't feel like family. He is in Position 2—important to his teammates, but emotionally distant.

Position 3 is in a halfway position, halfway up the cone and halfway toward the center. This represents someone who feels a moderate level of social indispensability. This worker doesn't feel fully indispensable, but doesn't feel socially useless either. So the Köhler effect is operating at a low level. The worker is moderately motivated. But this position can go either way—either climbing further up the cone or simply sliding back down. To reach their full potential, these workers need advanced delegation and team building strategies. When most of your people are in this position, your team has an "adolescent" culture. People are somewhat motivated but are not operating at their full potential.

This is perhaps the most common position in the workplace. Just think of a worker who has been a part of a team for a few years. She's pretty good at her job, and she knows everyone else in the office. But she feels like her job isn't very important—certainly not next to some of her other teammates. And she senses a clique of "popular people" that she doesn't belong to. She generally cares for her teammates, but she pulls away when they irritate her. She is halfway up Köhler's Cone, in Position 3—moderately impacted by the Köhler effect, but dangerously close to disengagement and stagnation.

Position 4 is at the top of the cone. This represents a worker who is doing the most important task that his position allows. And he works with a feeling of complete teamwork and camaraderie. This worker receives the full power of the Köhler effect, performing at a much higher level than if he worked in isolation. When many of your people are in this position, your team has an "extraordinary" culture. Every worker feels irreplaceable, and the whole team operates in full benefit of the Köhler effect.

Why does Köhler's Cone come to a point at the top? Because, as we've seen, the highest form of social indispensability is singular. It comes when there is a job that only you can do. Further down the cone, you are replaceable. Someone else could take your place and get the job done. But at the very top of the cone, there are no replacements. There is nobody who can bail you out if you can't perform. It's either you, or no one at all.

Does this mean that it's lonely at the top? Does the irreplaceability of Position 4 make workers feel isolated from their teammates?

Not at all! Each worker operates on his or her own cone, and the social indispensability of any two workers is not mutually exclusive. The irreplaceability of one does not inhibit the irreplaceability of another. Just consider the barbell lifters of Otto Köhler's study. Each of the three lifters felt equally irreplaceable to the team. Their social indispensability did not isolate them from their teammates—it bound them all together!

Don't think of Köhler's Cone like an organizational chart—where there's just one boss at the top and everybody else must accept a less prestigious position. Köhler's Cone exists in the mind of each worker. And it measures each worker's personal estimation of his or her own social indispensability.

Feelings of social indispensability are often influenced by the reality of the situation—as when someone is the last leg of an Olympic relay race. But people can also be mistaken. And throughout this book, we will argue that workers often feel less important than they really are. Your job is to push people up Köhler's Cone—both by changing the reality and also your workers' *estimation* of that reality. And you can do this with each of your team members—individually—so that everyone *feels* their own social indispensability. And when you push everyone to Position 4, your team will have a truly extraordinary culture.

This pays incremental rewards. You may be skeptical that this pinnacle of motivation can be achieved for every worker.

That's okay. Just view your motivation goals modestly. This will still make a huge difference. Every little bit that you push people up Köhler's Cone is helpful. For example, a worker at Position 3 has far more motivation than a worker at Position 1. And you can unlock massive amounts of performance just by bringing Position 2 workers even a few inches into the Social Circle. These small achievements make a big motivational difference and will contribute to an upward spiral of team performance.

And while the thought of pushing your most reluctant team members to the top of the cone may intimidate you, take heart. You can bring people to Position 4 in far more situations than you might expect. In fact, with the right leadership techniques, you can create these peak feelings of social indispensability almost anywhere.

CHAPTER SUMMARY

- Tasks can be important in two ways: 1) according to the necessity of the task, and 2) according to the degree to which the team depends on it.
- The position on the Task Triangle represents the objective necessity of a worker's task.
- The position on the Social Circle represents the level of team inclusion that the worker feels.
- Together, the Task Triangle and the Social Circle form Köhler's Cone.
- As you move up Köhler's Cone, you become more irreplaceable.
- The top of Köhler's Cone represents the peak position of social indispensability, where motivation is highest.

ACTION ITEMS

- What culture does your team currently have? Does it lean more towards a survivalist culture or a country club culture?

- Rate the relative strength of your past leadership style. Where are you strong, and where do you need the most improvement? (1 = no skill, 10 = extreme skill)?

The Task Triangle

    1   2   3   4   5   6   7   8   9   10

The Social Circle

    1   2   3   4   5   6   7   8   9   10

- List five tasks that seem easy to elevate on Köhler's Cone. These represent your low-hanging fruit that you can use to motivate members of your team (for example, "Ask Bob, who has technical expertise, to help during a software crisis.").

1. _____

_____

2. _____

_____

3. _____

_____

4. _____

   _____

5. _____

   _____

- List three tasks that seem most difficult to elevate up Köhler's Cone. These are the tasks that will test and develop your motivation skills. (for example, "Tweak the paperwork flow of HR documents.").

  1. _____

     _____

  2. _____

     _____

  3. _____

     _____

CHAPTER 10

THE CONVERSION

Crafting a Personalized Motivation Plan

Daniel was alone when he drove out to the Habitat for Humanity worksite.[26] It was his first time volunteering. He had called the local Habitat for Humanity office in Terrebonne Parish, Louisiana, and they told him to show up bright and early on Saturday morning. So he had woken up early and put on his work clothes, excited to do some meaningful work.

But when he showed up, he found chaos. The worksite was buzzing and crowded with volunteers. There were four or five houses under construction and several tasks happening at once: the installation of siding at one house, framing at another, and other building projects elsewhere. There were several large volunteer groups—one from a company, and another from a church. These groups formed cliques and even had personalized T-shirts that identified their organizations.

Daniel didn't have a special T-shirt.

He walked over to the orientation table and asked what to do. A volunteer coordinator gave him a waiver and then sent him over to one of the houses—the house where they were putting up siding. He walked over and saw the foreman hammering in a nail. When Daniel identified himself, the foreman paused briefly and said, "Go ahead and hold siding in that line."

So Daniel walked over to a group of six or seven people who were holding siding. Their job was to hold the siding in place so that the foreman and another seasoned volunteer could come by and nail the siding into the wall. It didn't take long to realize that this was an extraneous job. The foreman, along with the seasoned volunteer, could hang the siding just as quickly without the team of volunteers to idly hold it in place. In dissatisfaction, Daniel turned to the volunteers next to him, hoping to ask a question, but they were busy chatting amongst themselves. The topic was celebrity gossip. So Daniel turned back to his busywork, silently holding the siding so the experts could work.

This foreman was unwittingly breaking rule number one.

In the late afternoon, everyone gathered to celebrate their progress. The coordinator announced the accomplishments, and the foremen, sweaty and exhausted from work, beamed with self-esteem. They felt good because they had done meaningful work. But Daniel felt like a fraud, being celebrated for progress that he hadn't helped to bring about.

He didn't show up to the worksite the next weekend. He had lost all of his motivation to volunteer. After all, what was the point? Why would he waste another Saturday doing busy work? He stayed at home for the next several weekends, allowing his skills, his energy, and his goodwill to remain untapped.

But everything changed a few months later.

On a Tuesday morning, Daniel received a desperate call from the Habitat for Humanity volunteer coordinator. She needed help. There had been a problem with the scheduling, and the roof trusses were en route that day. But it was the middle of the week, and no volunteers were available. There were no church groups or corporate volunteers to come help. But the trusses were already on their way, and they needed to be installed before the roofing started on Saturday. So they were calling everyone in the area and asking for volunteers. But everyone was saying no.

Daniel said yes.

Even though it was Tuesday morning and he hadn't planned to volunteer that day, he drove out to the worksite.

When he arrived, he saw a much different scene than before. There were only a handful of volunteers, scrambling around a crane that held a roof truss high in the air. When Daniel approached the group, a foreman he had not seen before called out, "Are you here to help?" Daniel nodded, and the foreman replied, "Thank God!"

The foreman looked at him for a moment. "You're tall and fit" he said, "Are you comfortable driving in nails?"

"Yes," said Daniel.

"Show me," said the foreman. He handed Daniel a hammer, a nail, and a block of wood. After Daniel drove in the nail with a few swings, the foreman nodded. "Okay Daniel. We need someone to climb the walls and help guide the trusses into place. Otherwise, the trusses are going to be crooked, and we won't be able roof the house. We need you to climb up there, grab the truss as it's lowered, and guide it into place. When it's in place, let me know. Then drive in a temporary nail to keep it there. Can you handle that?"

"Yes sir!" said Daniel. And they got started.

Daniel worked all day with the small group of volunteers, scrambling atop the framed walls and helping to set truss after truss into place. Throughout the day, the volunteers grew more comfortable with Daniel and conversation arose naturally—often about the history and identity of the team members.

The work was challenging. Daniel's arms grew sore. His hands blistered. He worked until he could barely stand up any more. But the house now had trusses. They had finished the job. And Daniel went home happy and satisfied, feeling that he had done something worthwhile with his day.

But the story isn't over. Do you think that was the last time he ever volunteered for Habitat for Humanity? Of course not! That experience made him more determined to help. And so he came back—again and again. He started volunteering regularly, avoiding Saturdays and working with the weekday crew instead. They eventually gave him a T-shirt that showed he was a member of the crew. And the more he worked, the more his loyalty, his skill, and his motivation increased.

Eventually, after encouraging conversations with the weekday foremen, Daniel took the next step, enrolling in the Habitat for Humanity leadership training course to become a foreman himself. Think about that—this was the same man who, after having a negative experience on a Saturday, decided never to return. But now he was himself becoming a foreman. What had changed?

We can explain this with Köhler's Cone.

What went wrong when he showed up on that first Saturday? First, there was a failure of delegation. He didn't have an important job, or something that used even a fraction of his skills. Second, there was a failure of inclusivity. The Saturday foremen did not attempt to bring him into the fold, but instead let Daniel sit idly by and watch while others worked. So regarding

Köhler's Cone, Daniel was neither inside the circle nor up in the triangle. There was neither camaraderie nor necessity. There was no social indispensability. So the Köhler effect didn't activate. And Daniel left with no intention to return.

What changed? He received a desperate phone call! They needed help, and there was no one else available. He was their last hope. They needed him! Then, the weekday foreman met with him individually. He assessed Daniel, gave him a crucial task, and treated him like an important member of the team. The foreman brought him into the circle and pushed him up the triangle.

These are the two steps to bring someone up Köhler's Cone. This is how you make someone feel like an essential member of the team. You give them an important job, and you build social bonds with them. You bring them up the triangle and into the circle. You make them feel like a vital member of the team.

And now we need to address the practical question: How? How do you push people up Köhler's Cone? How do you establish social indispensability? How do you let them know that they are important members of the team?

That's where we turn next—to the first part of Köhler's Cone: the Task Triangle.

CHAPTER SUMMARY

- You can reengage workers with Köhler's Cone.
- Different leadership actions will elicit different responses from the same people.
- It's never too late to motivate people to extraordinary performance.

ACTION ITEMS

- Identify five people that you want to motivate and pinpoint their starting position on Köhler's Cone.

Person to Motivate	Position	Weakness: Triangle or Circle?
Example: Bill Johnson	*Salesman*	*Weak in the circle*

1. _____

   _____

   _____

2. _____

   _____

   _____

3. _____

   _____

   _____

4. _____

   _____

   _____

5. _____

   _____

   _____

PART III

THE TASK TRIANGLE

CHAPTER 11

CLIMBING THE MOUNTAIN

Making People Feel Important

The first half of Köhler's Cone is the Task Triangle. As we've seen, it illustrates a task's perceived importance. The more important someone feels their task to be, then the further up that person is on the Task Triangle. At the bottom, the member of the team feels the job worthless and extraneous. At the top, the worker feels necessary.

Recall the model from Chapter 9. If you want to activate the Köhler effect and unlock extraordinary performance, then you need to bring people up the Task Triangle.

The Task Triangle

It's absolutely necessary

Would hurt without it, but would survive

Nice, but wouldn't miss it

It's superfluous

But how does this happen? How do you make people feel that they have an important task? There are four steps.

First, you must assign jobs that are important. People can't feel important if they don't have crucial roles to play. Without these roles, they aren't even on the team. They are just observers. You wouldn't call them teammates. Teammates all have something to do. And the more valuable their jobs, the more valuable they feel. So they aren't going to feel important until you assign them the most valuable tasks that they can handle.

Second, you must communicate expectations. It is expected that important tasks will be done correctly. They can't be handled sloppily or delegated negligently. To feel valuable, people need to know what's expected of them, and that their tasks are worth doing correctly. They need a clear set of directions and operational boundaries. These are the things that distinguish one task from another, and that distinguish the important from the extraneous. And if their task is valuable, then it must have a clear identity—a clear definition. That makes them feel irreplaceable.

Third, you must communicate what is at stake. Important tasks are important for a reason. They mean something. They matter. They make the world a better place. Your workers won't feel valuable until they see the meaning of their work. What future are they helping to create? What goal are they contributing to? That's what you need to show them.

Fourth, you must offer assistance. Tasks can be difficult—all leaders know that. The level of importance of a task can be measured in a simple way. When times get tough and the worker calls out for help, does the leader respond? Is the task worthy of the leader's attention? If not, then the task must not be a high priority. But if the leader invests time and resources, personally getting involved to offer support, and putting it all on the line to ensure success—then the worker goes straight to the top of the triangle.

These are the four steps up the Task Triangle. 1) assign a task, 2) set your expectations, 3) communicate the stakes, and 4) provide assistance. To bring your workers to the top of the triangle, you need to fulfill all four steps.

The Task Triangle

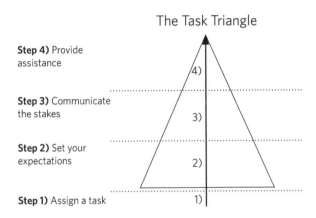

Step 4) Provide assistance

Step 3) Communicate the stakes

Step 2) Set your expectations

Step 1) Assign a task

Notice that these steps build upon each other. You assign a task before you set expectations. You communicate the stakes before assuming performance. And you provide assistance once your people have already begun working.

Here's how it might look.

First, you observe that a worker disengages because she doesn't feel important. So you consider her competence and assign her a new responsibility, selecting a vendor for your raw materials. This job carries significant risk, but it's nevertheless appropriate to her skill level. Now your worker has new life—a shot of energy. Her mind awakens to learn the new task and to establish a new equilibrium. She sees a need to grow. She is reengaging.

Second, you meet with her and tell her exactly what she needs to accomplish. You give her clear outcomes to achieve. For example, you tell her what margins are acceptable and the annual average price for the raw materials. You give her a goal and show her that it's realistic. Then you give her clear directions about how to achieve that goal, providing a sample negotiation template to use with the vendors. This allows her to distinguish valuable behaviors from those that are unimportant.

Third, you connect her new task to the bigger picture. If you can't get a good price for the raw materials, then you might have to switch to cheaper materials. This will reduce the quality of your product, which may possibly cause dangerous product failures. This gives gravity to the task. She realizes that she's not just ordering materials—she is ensuring a quality product. And that quality product is strengthening the whole economy. That is a big deal. So she rises to the occasion.

Fourth, you give her some help. You deliver the paperwork she needs to make purchasing decisions. You equip her with the latest purchasing software and send her to a negotiation workshop. When she encounters a crisis, you step in and help her, showing her how you've handled the situation in the past. She picks up on your belief in her. And she knows the job is important.

These four steps provide an outline for the chapters in Part III. Chapter 12 addresses the issue of assignment. Chapters 13 and 14 explore how to properly set expectations. Chapters 15 and 16 investigate how to raise the stakes for your workers and show them the importance of their tasks. And Chapters 17 and 18 discuss assistance and how to elevate the task through support.

This is our plan for Part III and our plan moving forward. Master the techniques found in these chapters and you will bring your workers up to the top of the Task Triangle, maximizing the first half of Köhler's Cone.

CHAPTER SUMMARY

- The Task Triangle is necessary so that the Köhler effect is activated.
- Members of the team need to know that their work is meaningful and important.
- There are four steps to reach the top of the Task Triangle: 1) assign a task, 2) set your expectations, 3) communicate the stakes, 4) provide assistance

ACTION ITEMS

- Rate the current attitudes of your team members. Answer each question as your team would respond (1 = disagree strongly, 10 = agree strongly).

1) Workers feel that their current job utilizes their full potential.

   1   2   3   4   5   6   7   8   9   10

2) Workers know what's expected of them and who they report to for every task.

   1   2   3   4   5   6   7   8   9   10

3) Workers consider their tasks to be meaningful and connect them to the greater good.

   1   2   3   4   5   6   7   8   9   10

4) Workers feel fully empowered and supported to execute their responsibilities.

   1   2   3   4   5   6   7   8   9   10

- List five things that you typically do to make workers feel important (for example, "Give financial bonuses at the end of a successful year.").

   1. _____

   _____

   2. _____

   _____

   3. _____

   _____

   4. _____

   _____

   5. _____

   _____

CHAPTER 12

THE EDGE OF COMPETENCE

Matching Workers to the Highest Tasks

T he first step in the Task Triangle is assignment. You need to give people an important job to do. You need to put a hammer in their hands.

Leaders hold a special position. From your place at the top of your team, you can see the connection between individual tasks and the ultimate goal. You assign tasks and delegate responsibility. This is the most fundamental task of business leadership: matching workers with the job that's right for them.

Your role is to give people the most important job possible, based on their level of competence. For example, if their competence is a level six, then don't give them a job with importance

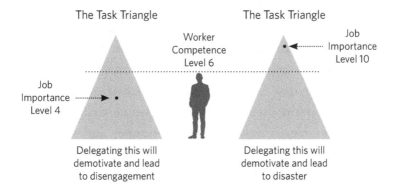

The Task Triangle

Worker
Competence
Level 6

Job
Importance
Level 4

Delegating this will
demotivate and lead
to disengagement

The Task Triangle

Job
Importance
Level 10

Delegating this will
demotivate and lead
to disaster

level ten. That leads to failure. Similarly, you shouldn't assign a task that's at importance level four, either. That will only disengage them. Instead, take them to the very edge of their competence.

If your people can handle level six tasks, then delegate them level six projects. But if they can comfortably handle level ten, then assign them level ten tasks. Köhler's Cone tells us that the more indispensable the job, the more effort workers will make. It's that simple. Later on, you're going to convince workers that their jobs are probably more important than they suspect. But for now, just delegate to them the most important tasks possible.

However, we've seen two common obstacles to matching team members with the job that's right for them.

1) Imbalance

Some leaders worry that there is an overabundance of low-level tasks. They see only a few level ten tasks but hundreds and hundreds at level two. They worry that if they delegate away too many level ten tasks, then the low-level tasks will go uncompleted.

There are several problems with this belief. First, low-level tasks are, by definition, less important than higher-level tasks. So it's much better to neglect something at level three than level nine. Focus on your most important tasks first, because these make the most significant contribution to your desired results.

Remember that we're using importance as our standard—not social prestige. It's a mistake to assume that low-paying tasks always have a low-level of importance and highly-paid tasks always have a high-level of importance. In reality, they are often unrelated. For example, we've met several highly paid executives who spend most of their time with unimportant tasks—attending bureaucratic meetings, mindlessly signing off on one another's projects, and playing afternoon golf. These tasks, although considered prestigious, have an extremely low level on the Task Triangle. But just imagine what would happen if the garbage workers stopped removing garbage. The whole community would grind to a halt!

As a leader, you need to see tasks for their true importance—unbiased by popular stereotypes. Pierce the veil of prestige and evaluate tasks independently of their reputation. Evaluate each task objectively, according to its actual contribution to your team's goals. This will become necessary later when you communicate the importance of a worker's task. But you must first identify true importance for yourself.

Second, leaders need to remember the natural variety of competence among their workers. It's uncommon for people to have achieved a competence level of ten. It's much more common for people to be at a lower level.

Think of it like pull-ups. Some people can only do three consecutive pull-ups. But it's less common for people to be able to do ten. Why? Because it requires more fitness to complete ten. Does that mean that people who can only do three pull-ups are stuck at three forever? Of course not! They can improve over time. But here's the point: if you can only do three consecutive pull-ups, then you will feel perfectly satisfied after doing three. You will feel proud of yourself. It will represent a full engagement of your fitness.

So when you delegate tasks, assign ten pull-ups to the people that can do ten, and three to the people that can do three. Afterwards, both groups will feel equally satisfied with their achievement, even though it's different amounts of work. For both, it represents the maximum that their current competence allows. They have both maxed out.

When it comes to an overabundance of low-level tasks, don't worry. There are plenty of people who will be quite satisfied with jobs that others would find tedious. Focus on matching people with the highest possible tasks that they can do. That's the real challenge. If you do this correctly, you will have no trouble filling the lower-level jobs.

If, for some reason you can't find people for low-level tasks—especially those that are low in prestige—then you should put the task on your personal to-do list. Think of a good foreman on a Habitat for Humanity worksite. He gives his hammer to a volunteer and lets her drive in nails while he sweeps the floor. He gives away the higher level task and takes the lower level task for himself. That's true leadership.

Follow this example in your own team. Pull people up to their maximum level of competence and fill in the gaps yourself.

2) Insecurity

Some leaders hesitate to delegate because of fear. They fear that if their teammates take all of the important tasks, then they themselves might become obsolete. They worry that they might delegate away their relevance. So these leaders hold on to responsibility as a form of power. And they prevent the people they manage from rising to their highest potential. But this wrecks the Köhler effect, spreading demotivation and disengagement. And when performance drops, the leaders can't lead their team to success, thus putting their own jobs at risk.

These fearful leaders miss the whole point of leadership. Their job is to elicit high performance from their workers. But if leaders hoard power and leave potential performance untapped, then they compromise the results of their team. It's ironic when you think about it. These leaders' feelings of dispensability cause them to do the exact *opposite* of their job description. But there's nothing more dispensable than leaders who diminish the performance of their team!

Don't let this happen to you. Delegate all of the most important tasks—every single one of them. If you find a task that you believe no one else can handle, then do it yourself only until you can train someone else to take it over. Raise the general level of performance by empowering everyone to reach their maximum level of competence.

Are leaders like this at risk of losing their jobs for being extraneous? Quite the contrary! They receive promotions! They move to higher and higher levels of the organization. They become the most important and most indispensable people in the whole company. After all, they can elevate performance and match people to the highest, most important tasks. Investors want people like this to run their organizations. And these are the leaders that can build teams that workers are desperate to join.

So plan your delegation deliberately. Make a list of the tasks required to reach your team's goals. Then do two things. First, rank the tasks according to their level of importance. Then, identify the essential skills required to complete each task. For example, you might list "give sales presentations" as a task. First, rank its importance. Because your team is responsible for business development, you determine this task is an eight out of ten. Next, because your products are highly technical, you will conclude that workers need an exceptional product knowledge to complete the task.

On another piece of paper, list your team members. And next to each, write their relative competence in the relevant areas. For example, for the task of giving sales presentations, list three team members with their level of product knowledge. Bill has an average knowledge of the product. Amy has an exceptional knowledge, and Henry's knowledge is solid but somewhat outdated. This exercise will reveal who is best qualified for each task.

Lastly, make a decision. In our example, you decide to give Amy the responsibility for sales presentations. The job requires a strong product knowledge. She has it. When you give her the responsibility, she will feel more valuable—which will satisfy a condition of the Köhler effect.

But we haven't finished yet.

It's one thing to make a decision about delegation. It's another thing to execute it. Your delegation style will make a huge difference to the perceived importance of the task. Delegate tasks casually and haphazardly, and people will view the new responsibilities as a mere nuisance. But delegate wth gravity and purpose, and people take it seriously. They will rise to the occasion.

That's the subject of our next chapter.

CHAPTER SUMMARY

- Your job is to match workers to the most important job that the competence permits.
- Leaders must overcome insecurity and fears of imbalance.
- The most valuable leaders are those that delegate their most important tasks to others.

ACTION ITEMS

- List five important tasks and the people to whom you might delegate them.

Task to Delegate	Level of Importance	Assign it to (Which Person)
Example: Creating bids	*8.5*	*Sally Cotton*

1. _____

  _____

  _____

2. _____

  _____

  _____

3. _____

  _____

  _____

4. _____

  _____

  _____

5. _____

  _____

  _____

- List three low-level tasks that you yourself will take over to free up time for your more competent workers (for example, "reordering office supplies").

    1. _____

    _____

    2. _____

    _____

    3. _____

    _____

CHAPTER 13

THE UNMISTAKABLE MESSAGE

Delegating in the Common Language

The second step in the Task Triangle is to communicate expectations. When you assign someone a task, your style makes all of the difference. And if you confuse people or downplay the assignment, then your workers will no doubt disengage.

For an analogy, let's consider a classical Biblical story found in the book of Genesis.[27]

According to the story, a single language originally united all the people of Earth. Everyone communicated clearly and effortlessly, speaking with the same mother tongue. In their unity, the people decided to build a tower—a tower so tall that it would reach the heavens. It would later be called the Tower of Babel.

First, the people built a foundation, then built layer upon layer toward the sky. As the tower grew higher, God took notice. "These people are making tremendous progress," God thought. "With this level of unity, every goal is achievable for them."

Then, to stunt the efficacy of the people, he confused their tongues, giving them different languages. Suddenly, they could no longer understand each other. They bumbled their operations. They could no longer coordinate their tasks. They confused each other. And this prevented the progress from continuing. They never finished building the tower.

The people then scattered across the land, according to their languages, thus dividing the people into different nations. And this is the Biblical story of how separate languages came to exist in the world.

Now, let's treat this strictly as an analogy and use it to illustrate an important point.

For the sake of the metaphor, imagine that the ground floor represents the most basic, concrete level of communication. It's highly descriptive and practical language that's easy to understand. But as you climb the tower, you move further and further from the emphasis on individual features. You start communicating in the clouds, with vague language, and with concepts that have multiple meanings and interpretations.

When you communicate in this abstract[28] language, you risk a misunderstanding. And this can cause your progress to break down.

For example, imagine that you assign someone a task to go to the zoo and bring you back a mammal. That could mean almost anything. There's no way of predicting whether he will fetch you a zebra or a dolphin. Now suppose that you need a dolphin, but you only ask him to bring you a mammal. You would feel misunderstood if he returned with a zebra. That's what abstract language does. It leaves room for competing interpretations. It leaves room for confusion.

This is what happened with the Tower of Babel. As the tower grew higher, the workers began to miscommunicate with each other. Misunderstandings spread, and confusion reigned. It felt as if they were all speaking a different language. So the project fell apart.

And yet, there was no confusion at ground level, where they still all spoke the same language. There was no miscommunication. When they began construction, their pace was fast. Their progress was strong—so strong, in fact, that it surprised even God himself!

Apply this lesson to your leadership. When you put a hammer into your worker's hand, tell her *exactly* what you want her to build. Communicate your expectations in simple, descriptive language. Make your assignment so clear that a misunderstanding is impossible. And to achieve this, you need to speak in a common language—the simple language of concretes.

This brings up a common question. Concrete communication may work well for tangible tasks—such as laying bricks or plowing a cornfield. But what about tasks that are more conceptual by nature? Suppose, for example, that you assign your marketing team to create an ad campaign that appeals to millennials. How would you make this concrete? Wouldn't an overly descriptive request defeat the purpose of employing creative professionals in the first place?

Not when done properly. Remember, your goal is to elevate the importance of a task by removing ambiguity about your expectations. If the outcome is important, then people need to be clear about which outcome you expect. You need to communicate a clear, descriptive standard to evaluate the results. You want a dolphin—not a zebra—so abstract communication won't do.

Consider the ad campaign example. It's tempting for leaders to simply assign the task as it pops into their minds: "Create an ad campaign that makes our product more appealing to millennials." This leaves a huge room for misinterpretation. How would someone know if the ad campaign appeals to millennials?

What's the standard? One worker might think the advertisement appeals to millennials if his daughter likes it. Another worker might think it succeeds if it's visually similar to another popular millennial brand. When you ask for a mammal, you can't predict what you will get. The request is too abstract.

Communicate concrete expectations even when you delegate highly conceptual tasks. In the case of the ad campaign, tell your team to create a new ad campaign that scores at least 80% on millennial focus group approval scores. Or tell them that you want the print ad to perform at least 25% better in an A/B test against the current campaign. You can pick any concrete standard that you want, just give them a standard that everyone can understand.

Notice that you don't have to describe the particulars of the advertisement you want them to create. For example, you don't have to request specific colors or fonts—let the creative professionals handle that. But be absolutely clear about the results that you want. These descriptive expectations establish the importance of the task and increase the likelihood of positive outcomes.

These are substantial benefits. But if the advantages of clear expectations are so pronounced, why don't leaders communicate concretely more often?

Some leaders are lazy. Communication is natural to every human. But *skillful* communication takes work. It's difficult to express an idea unmistakably, and many leaders don't want to exert the effort. This laziness restricts their ability to lead and motivate their team members.

But far more common than laziness is blindness. Many simply don't realize that they communicate in highly abstract terms.

They spend all day thinking about high level concepts and so it feels normal for them to communicate in these same terms. Their language becomes abstract and they don't even realize it. But when they communicate, they produce confusion and disengagement. And they wonder why.

Recently, a group of executives had to learn this the hard way.[29] They were leading a tech manufacturing company, and they had crippling communication problems between their manufacturing people and the engineers.

Here was a typical example. The manufacturing people who worked with the machinery would encounter a problem—say, a machine that needed a new part—and they would alert the engineers. Once the engineering people learned of the problem, they went back to their numerical schematics and designed something new.

But this didn't solve the problem. It actually made it worse.

The manufacturing people couldn't read the numerical schematics. They were't trained as engineers, so they didn't know what they were supposed to do. They grew frustrated because it felt like they never received a clear answer from the engineers. So they didn't do anything. But the engineers grew irritated because they designed elegant solutions that the manufacturing workers ignored. So accusations and a general lack of productivity resulted. This problem threatened the company's competitive viability.

What was the problem? The engineers were being too abstract for the manufacturing workers. But it didn't feel that way to the engineers. They prided themselves on their accuracy without realizing that they communicated way over the heads of their manufacturing workers. They cared more about correctness than communication, and they couldn't grasp why they weren't being understood. They didn't recognize their own blindness, so they dug in their heels when conflict erupted—confident that the truth was on their side.

What was the solution? Was it a "meet in the middle" arrangement where the engineers spoke a bit more concretely, and the manufacturing people spoke a bit more abstractly? No, meeting in the middle didn't work. The solution that worked was that the engineers communicated in the language of the manufacturing people. They abandoned their abstraction for more concrete language. They went down the tower.

But isn't this unfair? Perhaps. But fairness is irrelevant. If the engineers wanted to be understood, then they needed to speak concretely. Why? Because while only the engineers understood abstraction, *everybody* understood the bottom of the tower. In a sense, the engineers were "bilingual," so it was they who needed to adjust. And once they did, tensions eased, problems were solved, and plant-wide efficiency resumed.

It works the same way with your team.

When your people can't understand your requests, they won't produce extraordinary performance. Just like the engineers, you need to delegate in concrete terms. It's okay to think abstractly and use high level concepts to construct your strategy. But when it comes to delegation, you need to translate everything into simple language. Use practical descriptions and check that people understand what you want. This will ensure a meeting of the minds. It will prevent confusion and show people that you genuinely care that the task is understood and will be completed. This brings people up the cone and helps to activate the Köhler effect.

CHAPTER SUMMARY

- Vague directions confuse and disengage workers.
- Simple, grounded communication elevates the importance of a task.
- Leaders skilled in abstract thinking must communicate on the level of those who aren't.

ACTION ITEMS

- Identify which of the following directions are more concrete:

Delegation A	Delegation B	
Ex: "Bring me the tool."	"Bring me the screwdriver."	*More Concrete*
1. "Come to work on time in the morning."	"Be at the meeting when the clock says 8 a.m."	
2. "Remove the rats from the zoo's office."	"Get the animals out of the zoo's buildings."	
3. "Fire Kevin today and send him home."	"Resolve the tense office atmosphere."	
4. "Make the sale."	"Send the official proposal to AMCE Corp."	
5. "Turn off the AJ153 machine."	"Power down the important equipment."	

- Write five delegation scripts in concrete language (for example, "Take the John Deere combine from the barn and harvest the entire west field before Friday.").

1. _____

_____

2. _____

_____

3. _____

_____

4. _____

_____

5. _____

_____

CHAPTER 14

FOLLOW THE YELLOW BRICK ROAD

Providing a Clear Path of Action

W hen Dorothy first arrived in the Land of Oz, she was confused. She knew what she wanted—she wanted to go home. But she didn't know how to get there. She didn't know which direction to go. She needed leadership.

That's what the good witch gave her—leadership and a clear action plan. "Just follow the yellow brick road," she told Dorothy. "You can achieve your goal if you just keep walking on the yellow brick road." And with this direction, Dorothy reached the Emerald City and achieved success.

This provides a valuable leadership lesson. There are two ways in which your communication needs to be clear. In the previous chapter, we explored how to be specific only about outcomes. That's part of the second step of the Task Triangle. But that's not the whole step. You also need to communicate directions clearly. You need to give people an unambiguous, step-by-step plan of action.

Researchers illustrated this in a study about a college food drive.[30] The study involved fund-raising for food donations. The researchers divided the students into two groups. Everyone in the first group received a very detailed request for donations.

They received an individualized letter asking them to donate. This letter included a list of exactly which foods to donate and a map showing where they could drop the food off. A few days later, the student received a reminder phone call.

The second group got a letter with much less detail, addressed to "Dear Student" rather than to the name of a specific person. This letter didn't ask for a particular type of food, and it didn't include a map to the donation center. These students also didn't get a reminder phone call.

As you might expect, the students from the first group donated more food.

But there was a twist. Before the letters went out, the students were ranked by their peers. Each student received a ranking according to what extent the student's peers expected that he or she would be willing to donate. Researchers put students with a propensity to give into one group and those with resistance into another. Let's call these the "natural givers" and "resistant givers."

As you can expect, the natural givers donated more than the students deemed resistant. So far, no surprises. But here is the interesting question: Which mattered more? The disposition of the students or the letter that they received?

Among the students who received the less-detailed letter, none of the "resistant givers" donated and only 8 percent of the "natural givers" donated. These are dismal returns. But among the students who had received the detailed letter, fully 25 percent of the "resistant givers" donated!

Think about what that means. First of all, detailed instructions brought the donation rate from resident givers from 0 percent to 25 percent. It wasn't the request itself, but the *style* of the request, that made the difference. In this case, they

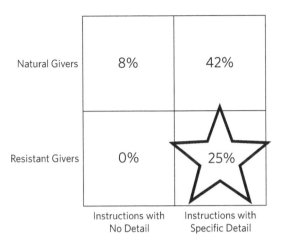

	Instructions with No Detail	Instructions with Specific Detail
Natural Givers	8%	42%
Resistant Givers	0%	25%

received detailed instructions. The researchers gave them a clear plan of action.

But what's even more significant is that these detailed instructions made "resistant givers" more than three times more likely to give than the "natural givers" who had *not* received clear instructions. The style of the delegation had more influence than a predisposition of compliance. Specifically, when sending a donation request, it was more important to provide a clear plan of action than to choose a receptive audience.

The same is true when you put a hammer in your workers' hands. Some leaders mistakenly believe that enthusiastic workers are more likely to perform than their less enthusiastic colleagues. But this simply isn't the case. Enthusiasm makes a difference—that's true. But a show of enthusiasm is far less critical than the clarity of your instructions. When people don't know how to take the next step, they hesitate. They procrastinate. And they are far less likely to perform than somebody who knows exactly how to proceed. When workers don't know what steps to take, they spend all of their energy and enthusiasm trying to figure out what to do. By the time they are ready for action, their emotional momentum has dissipated. And their performance will be low.

But when workers take action immediately—when they don't have to spend any energy figuring out what to do—then they give their best effort. They immediately start working toward their goal with a focused mind and no wasted steps. And as they start making progress on their project, they develop momentum, which further energizes them. Your clarity helps them to avoid premature fatigue.

This clarity also shows that you take the task seriously. You wouldn't give such specific instructions about a low-priority task, right? If you feel it's worth doing correctly, then it must be taken seriously. So your clear plan of action increases the perceived importance of the task. Workers approach the job with a greater intention.

So give the members of your team a clear plan of action. Describe the first steps they need to take to get started. Don't allow any chance for confusion. Tell people exactly what actions to take. The smaller, the better, especially with inexperienced workers. This will help them begin with a focused attack, which builds momentum for higher levels of performance.

For example, suppose you want your team of offshore fisherman to bring in a significant haul of seafood. As per Chapter 13, you set clear expectations: specifying bluefin tuna—not crab—and an outcome of at least fifty metric tons. Then you provide a clear path of action. "If it were me, I would start by sailing out to the Lonewood Islands," you tell them. "Then I would work my way back around the archipelago until the weather turns. If I didn't get fifty tons by then, I would head north into the Seas of

Distemper—which would be difficult sailing, but would probably help you reach fifty tons."

With these few words, you give them a default plan to follow. They don't need to scratch their heads trying to put together a strategy. You've outlined the steps needed to fulfill your request.

But what if they want to use a different strategy? That's okay, depending on their level of competence. Give your people the space to innovate and experiment with new strategies. Maybe that will lead to a new source of competitive advantage. But always give them a default strategy—something that has worked in the past that will enable them to fulfill your expectations. Don't force people to innovate every time you give them a hammer. Provide them with a clear path of action and allow them to innovate when their flash of inspiration hits.

But what if they already know the default strategy? Don't talk down to people or waste time telling them what they already know. Respect their competence and don't micromanage as a form of power play. Remember, your purpose is to make people feel important. So acknowledge the level of expertise possessed by your workers, adjusting your directions accordingly.

However, don't neglect to define a clear path of action. When you deal with a highly competent worker, simply *refer* to the first steps rather than explaining them. For example, instead of telling someone to, "Look up the number from the phone book, fill out a call plan, and put the number into the calling software," you can simply ask, "Are you going to use the call plan and the calling software?" In this way, you achieve a meeting of the minds without communicating any disrespect. And you will bring your workers up the Task Triangle without unnecessary explanations.

CHAPTER SUMMARY

- When people have clear directions, they are more likely to take action.
- A clear path of action is more important than the predisposition to perform.
- Most hesitation comes before taking the first step.
- The hardest part of success can be to get started.
- Make the first step easy, and your workers will gather momentum quickly.

ACTION ITEMS

- Identify the first step for five tasks that you plan to delegate:

Task to Delegate	First Step
Ex: Operation of the AXIS machine	*Open the control panel and prime the pump seventeen times*

1. _____

   _____

2. _____

   _____

3. _____

   _____

4. _____

   _____

5. _____

   _____

CHAPTER 15

THE LEADERSHIP SCOREBOARD

Making Motivational Information Public

W e've now reached the third step of the Task Triangle. We've already made assignments and communicated expectations. Now it's time to elevate the task. It's time to raise the stakes.

Recall the earlier research on athletes. What happened to the Olympic swim teams during the medley relay? When each swimmer swam with a different stroke, their performance didn't increase relative to their individual races. The Köhler effect failed to activate. Why was this?

Let's revisit the two observations we made in Chapter 8.

First, different strokes made comparison more difficult. When everyone used the same stroke, they could see how their score compared to those of their teammates. If they swam poorly, then everyone would immediately know. They would know whether their performance helped the team win gold, or caused them to miss the podium. And they would have to face the social consequences of poor performance.

But when they all swam different strokes, that immediate reporting was gone. Their performances were no longer an "apples-to-apples" comparison. Instead, it became like comparing apples to oranges. Teammates couldn't immediately recognize a poor performance—they first had to calculate the conversion of butterfly times to backstroke times, for example. This caused the problem. When performance is poorly recorded or vaguely understood, then people can't recognize relative performance. So the momentary feeling of importance decreases and the Köhler effect fails.

Second, not having a similar task allows people to hide their results. Teammates no longer have the ability to react instantly to someone else's performance. The more eyes on your task, the more important it feels. But when people don't know what you're doing, it feels less valuable. Workers don't have to face the immediate social consequences of poor performance. To that degree, people no longer feel accountable to their teammates, which drives down their feelings of indispensability.

So the crucial issue is for the whole team to have knowledge of its members' performances. This is accountability. But it's not good enough to have deferred accountability, where someone might only have to answer for their actions way in the future. That still provides plenty of room to hide right now. The Köhler effect depends on the current moment—the immediate, concrete present. Team knowledge has to occur as the action takes place. That's what happened with the weightlifters in Otto Köhler's original study. The three people on the same barbell knew immediately if one of the other lifters was giving a poor performance. The information was immediately available to the other teammates. So the Köhler effect was activated.

It's this public knowledge that triggers the Köhler effect. And used in this instance, we use the term "public" to indicate that knowledge is available to the other team members, not to the media or to society at large. Make the reality of your teammates' performances known to the rest of the team. This reinforces the indispensability of the task.

There are three ways to bring immediate, public knowledge into your team.

1) You can work next to each other. You need to observe each other work. That's what the barbell lifters did in the study. They worked next to each other and immediately saw when another lifter's performance changed. They didn't need reports or financial statements. They experienced it while it was happening. The knowledge was made public by their very presence.

This is easy if your team spends a lot of time together working on similar tasks. Working in someone's physical presence naturally puts you in a position to observe changes in their performance. And if everybody works in the same space, then the knowledge of everybody's work will be public to everyone. This provides the accountability necessary for social indispensability.

What might this look like outside of athletics? You could all work on the same assembly line and observe which people bottleneck the workflow. That's public reporting at its most basic. Or you could all chop wood and see the relative size of each person's pile. These tasks naturally lend themselves to real-time knowledge. So you merely need to perform these tasks in the presence of your other team members to trigger the Köhler effect.

2) But what if you can't bring everybody together to work in the same space? That brings us to our second strategy: record their performance. Recorded performance is hard to hide. Just ask Olympic swimmers. When you record performance, people can track it from all over the world. Consider the stock market. You don't need to be on the trading floor to know how stock prices are changing. The movements are recorded and immediately broadcast to anyone who is interested. So people

in Johannesburg and Tel Aviv both know exactly how the prices of their stocks are behaving. And they observe the changes the instant they occur.

This is the benefit of recorded performance: it allows you to extend the reach of your team's public knowledge. For example, you can display sales figures from teammates in remote areas in each other's offices. That way, each salesperson can see how they are performing relative to their peers. And if your goal is to reach a certain sales number for the group, poor-performing team members will work harder to keep from letting their peers down. They want to avoid the shame of being the weak link. That's the Köhler effect.

3) But what if everybody is doing a different job? This is the problem that the Olympic swimmers faced in the relay medley. To solve this, we need to turn to our final strategy—standardization. What does this mean? When you standardize performance you judge different actions according to a common standard. You normalize them to a single unit of measurement. This helps you solve the apples-to-oranges problem.

For example, you can't meaningfully compare a number of lemonades sold to a number of cars washed. That's not helpful. But you can assess both of them according to the amount of profit each generated. The actions of selling lemonade and washing cars are very different. One involves fixing drinks, and the other washing away dirt. But profit is a universal language for both. They both convert their action to profit. And so it's meaningful to compare the relative profitability of each.

Do the same with your team. Use a common standard to compare performance. If profit works well for you, then use it. But there are many other options. For example, you can use "customer service ratings" or "performance relative to a benchmark." Whatever you use, normalize the diverse performance of your teammates so that others can see how well they are performing. That will make people feel like indispensable members of a team. And that will activate the Köhler effect.

Some leaders worry that mutual accountability discourages morale. "Sure, it might boost performance," they acknowledge. "But for how long? And at what cost? What good is public information if it rips your team apart?"

Luckily, this blow to morale doesn't have to happen.

Researchers studied this in a nonclinical business environment.[31] They divided 460 management personnel into teams of four to five people to complete standardized business projects. Then they put every team into one of two groups, which were identical in every way but one. They told teams in the first group that they would evaluate both individual and team performance and report the results to their immediate supervisors. The second group received no such accountability, and hence had the expectation that their performance would neither be recorded nor posted for anyone to see.

Did it make a difference? You bet it did.

When the researchers tallied the results, the teams in the first group—the group where information was recorded and reported—experienced higher success in their projects. But they reported that even though they worked more and achieved more results, the work wasn't torture. The teams in the first group achieved success by relying heavily on their teammates. When everyone in the team was accountable to the same standard, everyone stepped up to contribute. The Köhler effect was activated. And these teams produced better results than those in the second group.

But did this tear the teams apart? Did the added pressure trigger conflict and lower morale? Did the public reporting turn workers against each other?

Absolutely not. Workers in the first group expressed more satisfaction with their peers than those in the second group. The recorded performance strengthened their social bonds, causing no conflict or cutthroat team politics.

This teaches us something important. If teammates turn against each other, it's not the fault of public knowledge. There is nothing inherent in records and reporting that encourages low morale. But if low morale already exists, then public reporting can aggravate the issue.

This is not a question of the Task Triangle—it's an issue of the Social Circle. It's not the task itself, but the team dynamic surrounding it that determines the consequences of making information public. You need strong bonds of teamwork to protect against conflict and feelings of alienation. Without those bonds, your people can feel crushed under the weight of their jobs. The Köhler effect won't operate without each member feeling that he or she belongs to the team. They need to enter the Social Circle. But we will return to this issue in Part IV.

For now, let's continue on to another way to raise the stakes.

CHAPTER SUMMARY

- Poor information management can cause the Köhler Effect to fail.
- When team members feel that they can hide poor performance, their level of performance drops.
- Recorded performance feels more important to the team than that which is unrecorded.
- Public knowledge of performance holds workers accountable.

ACTION ITEMS

- List five ways to make performance public within your team (for example, "Post performance on weekly/monthly company newsletters.").

  1. _____

  _____

  2. _____

  _____

  3. _____

  _____

  4. _____

  _____

  5. _____

  _____

- Brainstorm five ways to standardize performance between different jobs (for example, "Measure salespeople, mechanics, and office assistants with the same 'customer service' score.")

  1. _____

  _____

  2. _____

  _____

3. _____

_____

4. _____

_____

5. _____

_____

CHAPTER 16

POINTING UP

Painting the Big Picture

Several years ago, we worked with an oilfield chemical company.[32]

Their frontline techs delivered and applied chemicals to oil wells—chemicals such as demulsifiers, and corrosion inhibitors. These were experienced techs. But their workload was excessive. Every phone call was a crisis—maybe from a collapsed well or a chemical spill. So they stayed in a state of emergency, constantly pulled in all directions at once.

Over time, this took its toll.

When we met with the group, they were downtrodden, demotivated, and exhausted. They barely took note of each other anymore. Under the constant stream of crises, they had grown numb. They didn't feel like they were making any difference. Their jobs felt urgent, but not important. They were just zombies reacting to orders. And their performance was suffering because of it.

We recognized this immediately.

So we showed them how important their jobs really were. We connected the dots for them. And it caught them off guard when we did.

Bob: "I just want to take a moment to thank you guys for working so hard."

Workers: "Why? You have your own business. Our work doesn't affect you."

Bob: "Of course it does! And I really appreciate all the work you've been doing."

Workers: "How does our work make any difference to you?"

Bob: "Well, for starters, I drove here and that required gasoline."

Workers: "So? What does that have to do with us?"

Bob: "Well I don't know how to pump and refine gasoline to put into my gas tank."

Workers: "Neither do we."

Bob: "But the people who pump the oil don't know how to keep their pipes from corroding. That's what you guys know how to do. And if their pipes corrode, then they can't get the oil up and I can't put gas in my tank."

Workers: (Silence)

Bob: "You keep the pipes from corroding, which allows the pumpers to get the oil. That allows me to put gas in my tank and run my business. So you really are helping me. Thank you."

At that moment, it was as if a light had turned on. As we spoke, they started thinking about other things that they did, such as driving the local economy and reducing America's dependency on foreign oil. As they spoke, their posture began to improve, and the energy returned to their voices. They felt a sense of pride—even passion!—for the very jobs that they had previously hated. And it was all because they had started to understand the true importance of their tasks.

But they hadn't seen it on their own. We had to connect the dots for them. We had to show them the big picture. And we had to connect it all the way back to their daily tasks. It was this chain that finally helped them grasp the importance.

As a leader, you need to master this skill. You have the big-picture perspective that your workers may not have. It's your job to explain the importance of their tasks. You need to raise the stakes.

There are two parts to this. You need a vision, and you need to connect that vision to their tasks. You need the higher perspective and the narrative about how people contribute to the greater good. Give people a big picture without a connection, and it's irrelevant. Connect the dots without giving them a bigger picture, and you just confuse them. It only works if you give them both.

The first step should be the easiest. In theory, it's not difficult for leaders to see the big picture. After all, you sit at the top. You are free from the distractions of frontline tasks, and you can observe everything from a distance. You can see the sum of all the activity. Your team members are responsible for individual tasks, but you are responsible for the work as a whole. So your position of leadership should, by its nature, provide you with the big-picture perspective.

But that's not enough. You must be able to communicate that vision. Articulate it. Transfer it from your brain to another's. Give them a story that starts with the greater good and ends with their next assignment. That's how you give them context. It's not enough to only see the big picture. You must be able to paint it so that others can see it, too.

Allow people to see the big picture by answering the following questions:

- What ultimately changes in the world as a result of their work?
- Who ultimately benefits from their work (such as customers, team, society, or family)?
- How does their work ultimately make the world a better place?

Provide answers to these questions and gather evidence for your claims. It's a mistake to try to inspire people with ideas that aren't grounded in reality. That may work for awhile, but it will ultimately backfire. When people discover that your big picture has no veracity, then they will become even more disheartened. Avoid this by sticking to the truth. Don't tell people that their job is curing cancer unless it is. Find the real value that your team creates. And then communicate that value passionately.

When you paint your vision, use small brush strokes. Remember, you're dealing with people who are stuck in a small-thinking mentality. Your vision won't work if you start out by feeding them a huge abstraction. Start on their level. Use vivid, concrete language. Meet them wherever they are. Then paint in the details of your vision over time.

Once you communicate the big picture, you need to connect it to their work. Show how their actions directly impact the greater vision. Help them see the chain of events—the ripple effect—that goes from their action to the grand scheme. Otherwise, your vision will fall flat, and people won't get any traction. Their job won't feel important, even when it is.

So make the connection clear. You won't win points for subtly. Make the connection obvious. Hit them over the head with it. Work backward, one step at a time, until you have a continuous line between their current tasks and the overall big picture. This is how you connect the dots and show people the importance of their tasks. That's how you push them up Köhler's Cone and transform them into extraordinary performers.

CHAPTER SUMMARY

- The big-picture perspective lends more importance to a task.
- You are in a better position to see the big picture than your team members are.
- For workers to see how their task connects to the big picture, you must show them.
- The big picture is most effective when workers see the chain of connection to their individual tasks.

ACTION ITEMS

- List five ways that tasks by your team contribute to the importance of the big picture (for example, "When US automotive manufacturing workers run quality control tests on their seat belts, they are helping to save more than 250,000 American lives.").

1. _____

   _____

2. _____

   _____

3. _____

_____

4. _____

_____

5. _____

_____

- Take a single task and connect it, step-by-step, to the big picture (for example, "When you sweep the sidewalks, you make the neighborhood look cleaner, which drives up property values and gives children in the district a better education.").

_____

_____

_____

_____

_____

_____

_____

_____

_____

_____

_____

CHAPTER 17

EXAM PREP

Helping Your Workers Succeed

It's time to conquer the last step of the Task Triangle. You've raised the stakes for your workers and communicated expectations about an assignment. You've made the task feel important. But now it's time to put your money where your mouth is. Now you need to offer assistance.

At a small-town high school, there were two calculus teachers. These two teachers had very different teaching styles. The first teacher, Mrs. Johnson, told students to read the whole textbook right away. Then she gave comprehensive exams without warning. Was it difficult? Extremely. But she felt that she was weeding out the weak students from progressing too far into the program. "Better that they fail now," she thought, "than to pursue mathematics in university and fail later. That would just force them to restart another program from square one. Better that they learn this lesson early." So Mrs. Johnson gave extremely difficult exams and saw student failure as proof positive that she was doing her job.

But Mrs. O'Brien had a different philosophy. She assigned the same calculus textbook that Mrs. Johnson did, but she tested the students on only one chapter at a time. And when she covered the material, she emphasized the sections that were most important. She told her students what to expect on the exams, providing study guides and practice tests. She wanted to make her students as familiar with the material as possible. She wanted them to learn it. She wanted everyone to get an A. And she considered student success to be proof positive that she was doing her job.

Now here's the simple question—which teacher would get the best performance from her students? Certainly, extraordinary students could thrive in Mrs. Johnson's classroom. But it would be a disaster for ordinary students. They would get frustrated, angry, and eventually give up. She had given an unrealistic task to the students—to teach themselves the whole subject of calculus and prepare for a test on any aspect of it. That was too much for high-school level students. That was not a task that would motivate students to perform. For all but the most exceptional students, it was a recipe for failure. And in reality, that's what Mrs. Johnson expected. She expected to weed out the unworthy.

The students in Mrs. O'Brien's class had a completely different experience. She wanted them to win. She delegated realistically sized tasks and then helped the students to succeed. She made it as easy as possible for her students to learn the material and to get an A. Of course, not all of her students got an A. But that was not for lack of trying by Mrs. O'Brien. She did everything she could to help them achieve success. And then she built on each success with progressively more demanding exams.

What was the primary difference between Mrs. Johnson and Mrs. O'Brien?

Mrs. Johnson didn't believe in her students. She didn't think they could change. She was not trying to teach them. She was trying to separate the winners from the losers. And if students couldn't handle her teaching methods, then she considered them losers. She made quick decisions about them and used their failure to justify her opinions.

But Mrs. O'Brien believed in her students. She provided them with incremental steps to help them win. And she believed that any high school student could learn calculus if they learned it through a series of small steps. She believed in their potential. And she made it easy for them to have that same self-belief in themselves.

These strategies communicate very different messages about importance. When the leader doesn't invest in someone else's success, it makes success seem either unimportant or impossible to achieve. And we've seen this same dynamic happen countless times in the business world.

A manager delegates a task. For example, he assigns someone the job to dig a trench. Then he gives his worker nothing to help with the job—no tools, no training, and no supervision. So the worker makes a few attempts to dig the trench without making much progress. Then he looks to his manager for support. When no support comes, the worker downgrades the importance of the task. "It must not be that important. Maybe this was something he just wanted me to do if I got all of my other work done. After all, how important can it be if it gets none of his attention?"

The worker neglects the trench and does other work. A few days go by, and nobody says anything. A couple of weeks pass, and nobody seems to mind. Then when the manager finally shows up to inspect the trench, nothing has been accomplished. He didn't realize that his neglect communicated unimportance—reducing the worker's feelings of social indispensability!

To achieve the opposite, you must do the opposite. Mimic the strategies of Mrs. O'Brien. Recall that she gave her students attention and told them how to succeed. She spent time teaching the material and preparing her students for the exams. And her students got better grades than Mrs. Johnson's students did. As a manager, you can do the same thing.

First, give your workers all of the supplies they will need. Don't ask them to dig a trench without handing them a shovel. If you aren't willing to invest in the necessary supplies for a task, then you must not think it's that important. The same applies to supplying shoddy, outdated equipment. The most important tasks get the best equipment. So put your money where your mouth is. If you want people to feel that their job matters, then give them everything they need to execute it. And give them the best tools, as promptly as possible.

Second, provide training. If a task is mission critical, then you can't afford to have inexperienced workers responsible for it. Would you let an untrained worker install the firing pins for a nuclear warhead? Of course not! Why? Because failure would mean the deaths of thousands— perhaps millions—of people. It would put the whole nation—the whole free world—at risk. The stakes are huge. So you would make sure you gave the worker as much training as possible. It works the same way in the business world. When you invest in training, you elevate the importance of the task. You push people up Köhler's Cone. Whether it pays for technical training or training for soft skills, every dollar you invest in training increases you team member's estimation of a job's importance.

Third, check in. If a task is important, then you can't afford to let it go unattended. You can't afford to let things fall too far behind schedule. You must make sure everything moves forward smoothly. You can't neglect it. In fact, neglect is the surest way to demonstrate that you do not value a task. To establish importance, check in on your team's progress. That said, make sure to tailor your supervision to the experience of your workers. If they are quite inexperienced, then you will need to check in early and often. But if a worker is highly competent, then you only need to check in occasionally. Either way, let your workers know that you are paying attention to their work. Let them know you are interested in their progress. Let them know that you are there to support them.

Doing these things will send a clear message to your workers that you want them to win. You want them to succeed and execute the task correctly. This not only makes the task seem important, but it also shows that you believe in your workers! You believe in their ability to complete these tasks and contribute to the team effort. This builds their self-confidence. You show that they are worth your investment and your support. They are worth your time and resources. And this pushes them up Köhler's Cone.

As you help your people, be careful of one thing. Sometimes workers will try to delegate a task back to you. On the surface, they seem to be asking for help. But actually, they want to abdicate responsibility.

It works like this. Suppose you ask Kyle to create a proposal. You get him all of the best computers, reports, and industry trends. You send him to professional training for proposal creation. And you check in with him regularly to keep the assignment relevant. So far, so good. You're doing everything right.

But then he asks you again how to do the job. He wants another demonstration. When you hand the task back to him, he drags his feet. Then he starts listing all of the reasons that you should do it. After all, you're more skilled. And he's better suited to the tasks he's already familiar with. He's unsure about his abilities, so he wants you to take back the lion's share of the work.

Don't fall for this. Remember the lesson from Habitat for Humanity: don't hold the hammer. It's good to help your people succeed. But it's a disaster to try to succeed *for* them. You will only disempower your workers and deactivate the Köhler effect.

When people try to delegate a task back to you, be ready. Acknowledge their concerns and continue to provide support. But don't allow them to give the responsibility back. Reaffirm their ability to succeed and your willingness to help them. But make it clear that they own the task. A demonstration of proper technique is fine, but doing the whole project yourself is not. After all, a high school calculus teacher can do a lot of things to help her students succeed. But the moment she sits down and takes the test for them, she loses her job.

So follow the example of Mrs. O'Brien. Support your people. Make it as easy as possible for them to succeed. Invest your time and resources into their development. Equip them with the right supplies. Train them in the best procedures. Help them believe that they are capable of doing the job. Then, be patient until they start flourishing. This approach will cause massive improvements in their motivation.

CHAPTER SUMMARY

- A leader's support greatly impacts the success of the workers.
- Neglect communicates the unimportance of the task.
- When you try to help your workers to win, they usually do.

- The three critical areas of support are 1) supply your workers, 2) train them, and 3) check in with them
- Some workers will try to delegate a task back to you. Don't let them.

ACTION ITEMS

- Rate the support you give your workers in the three key areas (1 = no support, 10 = total support)

Supplies

1 2 3 4 5 6 7 8 9 10

Training

1 2 3 4 5 6 7 8 9 10

Check-ins

1 2 3 4 5 6 7 8 9 10

- List five actions you can take to help your workers succeed (for example, "Buy new office chairs.").

1. _____

_____

2. _____

_____

3. _____

_____

4. _____

_____

5. _____

_____

- List five tasks that workers most often try to delegate back to you (for example, "filing expense reports.").

1. _____

_____

2. _____

_____

3. _____

_____

4. _____

_____

5. _____

_____

CHAPTER 18

MORE THAN A PICTURE

Demonstrating Proper Technique

What's the best way to make a task seem important? Most leaders attempt it through verbal communication. And that's a strategy that so far we've been assuming you're using. But actions speak louder than words.

What does this mean? It means that you don't just *tell* people what to do. You *show* them. You set the example through modeling the correct behavior. You step into the fire and show them how it's done. And then you invite them to follow your lead.

A great example of this comes from 1944, during World War II. The Nazi war machine had nearly conquered the globe. For years, the Allies struggled to halt the Nazi's ceaseless expansion into new territory. But to stop the Nazis, their stranglehold on Europe had to be broken. This was no easy task, for the Nazis had transformed the continent into a fortress, installing stalwart military defenses along the perimeter. To breach these fortifications, the Allies organized the largest amphibious assault in the history of humankind, landing nearly 5,000 military transport ships on the beaches of Normandy on D-Day, and successfully giving the Allied army a foothold in Europe.

But that was just the beginning. Then, the soldiers had to fight their way across the Nazi-occupied continent in a campaign with so grand a scope, it could only succeed with an abundance of heroic leadership. And the warfare that followed D-Day provided many examples.

Consider the following story of a brigadier general, as recounted by the historian Stephen Ambrose concerning events that took place during June 1944.

> Brid. Gen. Norman "Dutch" Cota, assistant division commander of the 29th, came on a group of infantry pinned down by some Germans in a farmhouse. He asked the captain in command why his men were making no effort to take the building. "Sir, the Germans are in there, shooting at us," the captain replied. "Well, I'll tell you what, captain," said Cota, unbuckling two grenades from his jacket. "You and your men start shooting at them. I'll take a squad of men and you and your men watch carefully. I'll show you how to take a house with Germans in it." Cota led his squad around a hedge to get as close as possible to the house. Suddenly, he gave a whoop and raced forward, the squad following, yelling like wild men. As they tossed grenades into the windows, Cota and another man kicked in the front door, tossed a couple of grenades inside, waited for the explosions, then dashed into the house. The surviving Germans inside were streaming out the back door, running for their lives. Cota returned to the captain. "You've seen how to take a house," said the general, still out of breath. "Do you understand? Do you know how to do it now?" "Yes, sir."
>
> Stephen Ambrose, Citizen Soldiers[33]

When Cota came upon that group of infantrymen, he could have just told them to take the house. He could have instructed them, using concrete language and outlining a clear plan of action. But these men had already been trained. They already had their orders—they didn't need to be told what to do.

So Cota did something else. He *demonstrated* how to take a house. He set an example, showing them exactly what he wanted. They watched him throw the grenades and charge the house. They saw him chase away the Germans and put the property back under Allied control. So when he returned, he didn't have to explain much. He had communicated what was essential with very few words. And he gave his soldiers a motivational example to follow.

Why was this example so powerful?

First, the infantrymen didn't have to struggle with his meaning. They didn't have to strain to understand anything. They just watched and saw what they were to do. They didn't need to understand any words of instruction. They just needed to open their eyes. The demonstration made their assignment simpler and less difficult to comprehend.

Second, they learned more information from watching than they could from hearing. A picture is worth a thousand words, but a demonstration is worth a million. For every task, there are a thousand possible ways to execute it, and a thousand potential questions that a beginner might ask. But when you demonstrate, you provide a concrete example of what will be required. You address uncertainties that haven't even developed yet. You give them a torrent of information in a form that's easy to digest, allowing the witnesses to begin with a strong foundation of knowledge.

Finally, they see that achieving the goal is possible. They don't have to worry about being on a wild goose chase. They don't have to speculate. They know that the task is realistic. They have seen it. You made it look easy. So they can easily believe that they can do it, too. After all, they are not that different from the leader. And if they run into trouble, they can always look to the leader for help. The same person who set the expectations demonstrated that it is possible, giving people the confidence to take the first step. That's the power of the leader's example.

When you demonstrate the task, you send a clear message of its importance. If the leader is willing to devote time and energy to it, then it must warrant respect. It must be worth a lot. So workers will approach the task with more respect. And this will bring them high up on Köhler's Cone, unleashing strong reserves of motivation.

When you first assign a task, demonstrate it. Perform it in front of your workers, in their presence. Use it as a teaching moment. Tell people why you perform it in a certain way. Make yourself available to answer questions. Perform the task several times, if necessary. Then hand it off to your workers. This will give them a solid foundation upon which to start their work.

But once you've done that, your job isn't over. Check in with your workers periodically. Look for mistakes in their work or signs that their motivation is waning. These might indicate a slide down the Task Triangle. If this happens, step in and take on a few shifts. Show them that the job is important enough to warrant the leader's time. Show them the pace and the productivity that you expect.

Be like General Cota. Your people may know how one is supposed to take a house. But when you roll up your sleeves and do the dirty work, they approach the job with more gravity than before. They lose their excuses. And they feel motivated to follow your lead. That's why Teddy Roosevelt led the charge up Kettle Hill. And you can achieve the same results when you set a positive example for your people.

CHAPTER SUMMARY

- Verbal instruction is not the only way to communicate how to accomplish a task.
- Your directions are more powerful when you demonstrate them with your actions.
- People understand demonstrations more easily than instructions.
- Demonstration builds your leadership credibility.

ACTION ITEMS

- List five important tasks that you can demonstrate:

Task	Demonstrate to Whom?	By What Date?
Example: how to run a sales meeting	Kelly Hanover	3/31

1. _____

_____

_____

2. _____

_____

_____

3. _____

_____

_____

4. _____

_____

_____

5. _____

_____

_____

PART IV
THE SOCIAL CIRCLE

CHAPTER 19

JOURNEY TO THE CENTER

Bringing Workers onto the Team

We've reached the second half of Köhler's Cone. While the Task Triangle dealt with the importance of a task, the Social Circle is about the intimacy of your team. As workers feel more included, they move further to the center of the Social Circle. On the outside, they feel isolated and alone. From the center, they feel safe and connected.

Recall the model from Chapter 9. If you want to activate the Köhler effect and unlock extraordinary performance, you first need to bring people into the Social Circle.

The Social Circle

On the fringes   In the inner circle

Not on the team   On the team

How do you achieve this? How do you bring people onto your team? There are three steps.

First, you must create a team. It's not enough to just want teamwork. You need to build a team, creating the foundation upon which it can be established. People subconsciously scan for cues of team identity. And they constantly assess whether or not they are included. Don't leave any room for doubt. Don't leave your workers wondering. Draw a clear line in the sand and bring them into the Social Circle.

Second, you must orchestrate shared experiences. Once you put your team together, don't leave it in its infancy. You need to cement the bonds so it can grow. And this happens during the time you spend together. Some shared experiences cement the bonds of teamwork much more strongly than others. If you leverage the most potent of these experiences, then you will elicit intense amounts of loyalty from your workers. And you will draw them more deeply into the Social Circle.

Third, you must establish social responsibility. The Köhler effect activates only when workers depend on each other. And this dependence needs to be made clear. This is the source of the motivational gains. Workers make an extraordinary effort because their teammates count on them. Bring that interdependency to their attention. Make it explicit and use it to reinforce the workers' feelings of importance. This brings people into the very center of the Social Circle, making them loyal and devoted teammates.

These are the three steps into the Social Circle: 1) creating a team, 2) sharing experiences, and 3) establishing social responsibility. To bring your workers into the center of the circle, you need to accomplish all three steps.

These steps follow a natural progression. You can't make a person feel like part of a team without the building blocks of teamwork. With those in place, you can deepen the bonds with

shared experiences. With strong bonds in place, you can empha-
size the interdependency that you all share. In the end, you will
have extremely close, loyal workers.

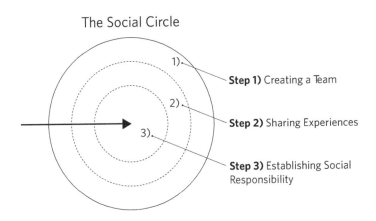

The Social Circle

Step 1) Creating a Team

Step 2) Sharing Experiences

Step 3) Establishing Social Responsibility

Here's how these three steps might look in practice: let's say
that you recognize that one of your workers feels isolated and
you resolve to make him feel more like a member of the team.
First, you communicate with him about the team. You tell him
where he stands as a valued member and give him proof to back
this up. You spend more time with him, choosing to work alongside him when your schedule permits. This begins changing his
perspective, and making him feel like he truly does belongs to
a team.

Second, you proactively create additional shared experiences. You invite the team member to lunch outside of the office
and then for dinner at your house. You jump in beside him as
he struggles to lift a heavy crate at work, grunting and sweating
beside him, high-fiving him once you put it into place. Over several weeks, these experiences begin to create strong social bonds
between the two of you.

Third, you highlight how the other members of the team depend on his work, and vice versa. You paint him a vision of the larger social consequences and show how he contributes to those consequences. As the team member begins to understand the power of the team, you give him leadership responsibilities, putting the worker in a position to shape the team's identity. This will bring him into the inner circle, inspiring the deepest levels of loyalty.

These three steps give us the chapters of Part IV. Chapters 20 and 21 explore the building blocks of team creation. Chapters 22 and 23 identify the experiences that are shared among your workers. And chapters 24 and 25 discuss how to bind your team together with the principles of social responsibility. The remaining two chapters provide an action plan for implementing the book as a whole.

This is our plan moving forward. Master the techniques found in the following chapters and you will bring your workers into the center of the Social Circle, maximizing the second half of Köhler's Cone. The Social Circle is the most commonly neglected component of Köhler's Cone, especially among ambitious leaders. This is your chance to set yourself apart from the competition. So let's get started.

CHAPTER SUMMARY

- The Social Circle is necessary for the Köhler effect to be activated.
- There are three steps to bring people into the Social Circle: 1) creating a team, 2) sharing experiences, and 3) establishing social responsibility

- Ambitious leaders have a tendency to neglect the Social Circle.

ACTION ITEMS

- Rate the current attitudes of your team members. Answer each question as your team would respond (1 = disagree strongly, 10 = agree strongly).

  1) Workers feel a clear team identity and clearly accept each member of the team.

     1   2   3   4   5   6   7   8   9   10

  2) Workers build strong bonds through frequent shared experiences.

     1   2   3   4   5   6   7   8   9   10

  3) Workers clearly understand how their performance impacts their other team members.

     1   2   3   4   5   6   7   8   9   10

- List five things that you typically do to make your workers feel included in the team (for example, "Buy each worker a cake on his or her birthday.").

  1. _____

     _____

  2. _____

     _____

3. _____

_____

4. _____

_____

5. _____

_____

CHAPTER 20

WHEN IT FEELS LIKE A TEAM

Promoting Feelings of Teamwork

The first step for creating the Social Circle is simple: build a team. Establish a cohesive social group where your workers can feel they belong. This brings them out of isolation and into the realm of Köhler's Cone.

But this won't happen automatically. Leave it to chance and it may not happen at all. You've got to build it. And it starts in the mind, when you help people *feel* like members of a team.

At first, this step might seem unnecessary. Why would feeling like a team change the way adults execute a task? But research shows that even the slightest feelings of teamwork can dramatically affect a worker's performance.

In a recent Stanford study, researchers put people into a room and asked them to solve a challenging puzzle.[34] After some time had passed, the researchers gave them a note that contained a tip offering advice about how to solve it. The researchers wanted to know whether the source of the tip would make a difference to the performance of the participants.

Researchers had divided the participants into two groups. To the first group, they said that the tip came directly from the researchers. To the second group, they said that the tip came from another participant. Before the attempts to solve the puzzles began, they told the second group that, even though participants would work alone, they were on a "team" with their peers. When these participants received the tip, they were led to believe that it came from one of their "teammates"—another participant offering friendly advice. Then the researchers recorded how long it took people in each group to solve the puzzle.

But there was a twist: the puzzle was actually unsolvable. The researchers simply timed how long the participants were willing to persist, even though they didn't make any progress. This is a classic psychological technique to test people's perseverance, willpower, and willingness to endure difficulty.

So which group do you think worked the longest on the puzzle? You might think that the person providing the tip shouldn't make a difference. And in one respect, it's true that it shouldn't. Knowledge should be assessed independently of its source. But people don't always follow this rule—especially when the pressure is high.

You might also think that people would persist longer when the participants thought the tip came from the researchers. And this idea is plausible. After all, the researchers had authority. They were scientists, and they administered the puzzles. Surely if anyone knew how to solve it, it would be the professionals, right?

But that is not what happened. When the researchers crunched the data, they saw it was the team-oriented group that had performed better. When participants thought that the tip came from another participant, they persisted 48 to 64 percent longer. That's an extraordinary increase in performance!

But that was just the beginning. Afterward, the participants reported having more interest in the puzzle. They were more engrossed, grew less tired and—most interestingly—they performed better on the puzzle than their counterparts did. Then, weeks later, these participants chose to do 53 percent more work on a related task in a separate setting. These are astonishing and wide-reaching benefits!

So what's going on here? Why does a difference in the source of a tip produce such an extraordinary increase in performance, even when the tip is the same? In the words of one of the researchers, "The results showed that simply feeling like you're part of a team of people working on a task makes people more motivated as they take on challenges." In other words, give people even the slightest sense of belonging, and their work capacity shoots up.

So how do you create these feelings of belonging? How do you communicate that someone is a member of the team?

There are two significant ways, summarized by countless elementary school children giving presentations: you need to "show and tell." Let's look at these in reverse order.

First, tell people that they belong to your team. The research supports the importance of this. In the tip study, researchers told participants that they were members of a team. In the bike study from Chapter 8, researchers told participants that their scores would contribute to a team score. Humans are verbal creatures. Words make a difference. So explicitly acknowledge their place on the team. It's simple to do, but also easy to forget. Don't neglect it.

Use phrases such as:

- "We're on the same team."
- "You're a solid member of our team"
- "Our team wouldn't be the same without you"
- "We're counting on you"

Give voice to these sentiments early and often. Tell people exactly where they stand. Leave no doubt in their minds. Tell them that they belong on your team.

Second, show people that they belong to your team. Do you remember when Daniel first arrived at the Habitat for Humanity work site? Everyone else had team shirts that announced their belonging. But Daniel only wore a plain T-shirt. This accurately reflected Daniel's exclusion from the team—at least in his own mind. But after consistently volunteering on the weekday crew, he received a crew-member shirt. And that meant something to him. It illustrated the fact that they had accepted him onto their crew. It showed that he now belonged to their team.

In the same way, you need to give people visual proof that they belong to your team. And you need to do it in several ways. Many simple but effective strategies are on the level of Daniel's T-shirt. These include items such as business cards, stationery, and official titles. These things work. Maybe they shouldn't, but they do. And they are too cheap and easy to overlook.

But the most powerful way to show people that they belong is through actions. People will respond to receiving the team jersey. But they will respond even more if you invite them to the exclusive team dinner. People notice your actions, and your actions send a powerful message.

So do the things that will make people feel like valued members of the team. Invite them to important meetings. Shake their hand when they enter the room. Spend time establishing a friendship. These things will quickly change outsiders into members of the team. And over time they will bring other people into the Social Circle, as well.

CHAPTER SUMMARY

- The Köhler Effect won't activate unless workers feel like members of the team.
- Feelings of teamwork significantly boost workers' performance.
- Leaders need to both "show" and "tell" to generate feelings of inclusion.

ACTION ITEMS

- List five things you can say during a conversation to create feelings of bonding (for example, "I'm with you through thick and thin.").

  1. _____

  _____

  2. _____

  _____

  3. _____

  _____

  4. _____

  _____

  5. _____

  _____

• Brainstorm three ways that you can *show* workers that they belong to your team (for example, giving out team shirts).

1. _____

_____

2. _____

_____

3. _____

_____

CHAPTER 21

GETTING THE GLUE TO STICK

Encouraging Overlapping Tenure

We're still on the first step of the Social Circle. We just explored the feelings of inclusion in a team and how to encourage them among your people. Now we need to ground those feelings. We need to discuss the concrete realities.

What's the first thing that every child learns about super glue? If you want the things you are gluing to stick to each other, then you have to press them together for a long time. If you give up too soon, then the bonds won't take, and the objects will eventually fall apart.

It works the same way with social relationships. If you want to establish a feeling of teamwork between yourself and other people—feelings that won't dissipate when the pressure gets high—then you need to spend some significant time with those people. You need to share experiences. And as you build feelings of team camaraderie, you move in the Social Circle and up the cone.

When you spend time with your workers, they trust you more. They begin to see you as a friend and ally. You generate strong subconscious associations of camaraderie even if you only work in proximity and only indirectly on the same project.

The more time you spend with your team members, the more likely is it that they will refer to you as "us"—as in "us versus them." And that feeling of "us" is the exact feeling of team identity that triggers the Köhler effect. It's the feeling that "we're in this together." And this feeling can start to take root when you spend time together.

One study looked at how this relationship worked within NCAA college basketball teams.[35] College teams differ from professional teams in that their players are students. They can only play on a team for a few years. An NBA team might have a franchise player who stays for decades. But this is impossible in college sports. Players can only play for a team for four years, at most. Then they lose their eligibility.

There is also another factor at play. Many college players are good enough to play on professional NBA teams. So instead of staying with their college team for four years, many quit and join the draft after only a single season. The temptation to do this further reduces the time that college basketball players spend together. It all adds up to a very fluid, "coming and going" culture on NCAA teams—a culture where teams frequently break apart after only a few seasons.

But even in this unstable environment, some teams are more stable than others. While some teams break apart after only one season, others start five seniors who have played together since freshman year. Some students leave for the NBA immediately, and others remain in the NCAA to pursue a championship. And there is a wide variation in between.

Researchers decided to investigate whether this time spent playing together factored into a team's success. They evaluated a sample of 230 NCAA men's basketball teams in the 2006–2007 season. And they measured two fundamental things. First, they ranked the skill of each player and coach. Second, they recorded each team's "overlapping tenure"—or, how many years the players and coaches stayed together. For example, if all the players on the team played together for all four years under the same coach, that would be the highest score of overlapping tenure. If 80 percent of the team changed every year, then that would be a low score of overlapping tenure. High overlapping tenure means everybody stayed together. A low score indicates that they broke apart after a short time.

The researchers compared this data to the actual performances of the teams. After they had run their analysis, several patterns emerged. First, they found that teams with the most talented players and coaches performed better during the season. That surprised no one. Everyone expected the level of talent to impact a team's success.

But the second finding was more surprising. They also found that performance increased alongside overlapping tenure. Even when you kept the talent of the players constant, time together as a single factor boosted a team's results. It wasn't that the players' skills increased by practicing together. Researchers examined talent separately. Instead, the shared experiences made players willing to work harder for each other. Just like the bonds formed by glue: the longer you hold a team together, the better they perform under pressure.

Use this principle when you lead. Encourage your team to spend time together. This comes in two forms. First, they need to spend time together in their daily routine, on a consistent basis. Second, they need to stay together over the long haul. You need both of these elements to make the glue hold for your team. So let's look at each of these individually.

1) Daily life

Help your team spend time together during the day. Start by setting your own example. Talk to people in the halls instead of just walking past them. Keep the door to your office open. Work in the conference room or in a public space where people can see you. Show your team members that you are one of them.

Make it easy for your team members to spend time together. Remove unnecessary barriers in their workspace, such as bookshelves and filing cabinets. Organize extracurricular activities. Run 5k races or attend team happy hours. Find creative ways to spend time together on a regular basis. This will strengthen the bonds of teamwork and allow the social glue to set.

2) The long haul

You also need to encourage workers to stay with the team long term. Depending on your industry, that could mean long-term employment contracts. Or it might mean that you keep the same personnel on the team together for different projects. But you don't need to rely just on formal strategies, like legally binding contracts. Use informal encouragement, too. Talk with your team members about their futures. Tell them that you want them to stay for a long time. Ask about their goals. Ask what it would take to win their loyalty into the future. Often a simple verbal agreement with a handshake will keep workers on your team for decades. Whatever your strategy, match it to your workers' personalities. Just make an honest effort to keep everyone on the team for a long time.

Remember, the goal is to produce feelings of camaraderie. So make the time you spend together pleasant. You can't always guarantee that circumstances will be good. But you can control how you treat people. If you attack your workers, or say things about them that are negative, then you will risk losing them. People are more sensitive to evidence *against* your team commitment than to positive statements that confirm it.[36] And according to the research by Dr. John Gottman, it takes about five positive interactions to outweigh each negative interaction.[37] And any negative interaction can potentially drive people away from the team and down Köhler's Cone.

It's critically important to treat people respectfully when you're together. Don't attack or criticize them. Be nice. Affirm their position on the team. Make them feel safe and valued. They will be more likely to commit to you after you first commit to them. Similarly, they will be more willing to commit to a team that they enjoy being a part of. So make the working environment pleasant. Give them positive associations with their jobs.

One of the simplest strategies is also one of the most neglected. And it will be the topic of the next chapter.

CHAPTER SUMMARY

- Teams are built, in part, by sharing time together.
- The more time you spend together, the better your team will perform.
- Workers need to spend time together on a regular basis.
- Long tenures together encourage better teamwork and greater results.

ACTION ITEMS

- Identify three workers with whom you spend too little time (for example, John Davidson in accounting).

    1. _____

    _____

    2.

    _____

    3.

    _____

- Identify five ways to spend more time with workers during the course of the day or week (for example, "Work from the open conference room once a week.").

    1. _____

    _____

    2. _____

    _____

    3. _____

    _____

    4. _____

    _____

5. _____

_____

- Brainstorm three strategies to encourage long-term tenure (for example, "Discuss a long term career plan for them with your team.").

  1. _____

  _____

  2. _____

  _____

  3. _____

  _____

CHAPTER 22

WHEN LIONS FEAST

Leveraging the Primal Traditions

W e've now reached the second step of the Social Circle. It's time to manufacture shared experiences that will cement people into the newly formed team. And for this, we can draw inspiration from nature.

Out in the African Serengeti, how can you tell which lions are in the same pride? The strategy is simple: watch them eat.

After they kill a gazelle, watch the lions that gather around it. If they all eat from the same gazelle at the same time, then they are probably from the same pride. It's that simple. If a rival lion approaches and tries to eat from the gazelle, what usually happens? The dominant male of the pride will stop eating, puff himself up, and chase the strange lion. Why? Because only the lions that bleed together eat together. Eating nourishes and strengthens the pride. And lions don't want the fruits of their labor to strengthen their rivals. So they only let their teammates eat from the gazelle.

It's not actually that different with humans.

Humans might dine with their enemies, but not usually. And even when they do, they might feel less antagonistic towards each other afterward. Why? Because eating together is a potent, primal bonding activity. That's one reason why first dates often take place at a restaurant. A shared meal strongly registers on your subconscious scale of bonding. The person who feeds you probably doesn't want to hurt you. So you start to trust them.

And this often translates directly into performance.

Researchers have tested this very thing. They looked at the dining habits of people who worked in fire stations.[38] Most fire halls have a kitchen that the members of the department are free to use. And when it comes to mealtime, there are two usual strategies.

Some fire stations have a custom of the firefighters cooking and eating their meals together. Each day is somebody else's turn to cook for the rest of the station. Everyone eats together at a large table and jokes about each other's cooking. And each person on the force rotates the responsibility to cook and clean for everyone else. It's a longstanding tradition.

But other fire stations don't do this. In these stations, every firefighter decides about his or her own meal. They are free to use the kitchen, but there is no rotation of group meals. Firefighters cook alone, bring their lunch, or go off to a restaurant to eat. It's just a difference of culture. At some fire stations, the firefighters eat together, and at others, they don't.

So here's the question: do dining habits make any difference to performance? To find out, the researchers compared thirteen fire stations and nearly 400 firefighters, looking for a connection. Guess what they found? Those stations that eat together are the highest-performing stations—regardless of their neighborhood or their resources.

The researchers stated, "Behavior that might seem superfluous or wasteful to outside observers ultimately carries significant importance for organizational performance." In other words, the experience of shared dining together builds trust and camaraderie, bringing them all deeper into the Social Circle. And this boosts motivation.

Eating together even impacts performance on the individual scale.

Researchers compared the performance of children from households that do and don't eat regular family dinners. They found that frequent family dinners are a better predictor of high achievement scores than creating art, playing sports, doing homework, or even spending time in school. Children who eat family dinners at least five times a week are twice as likely to earn A's in school than those whose families eat dinner together less than two times a week.[39] Once again, high performance correlates with the shared experience of eating—an activity that many leaders otherwise overlook.

How to apply this knowledge is obvious. If you want to motivate people, then eat a meal with them. This shared meal can take almost any form. But if you don't know where to start, begin with the business lunch. This is a quick opportunity for two people to bond in a way that they otherwise can't at the office. The same holds true for corporate dinners, where the whole team dines together, often in a completely different atmosphere than that of their workspace. Some managers employ this principle with so-called happy hours, where food (and not just drinking) is offered after work hours.

And of course, the most effective strategy of all is to invite somebody to dinner at your home. This most powerful of shared experiences is recognized the world over and treated with great respect by countless cultures.

When you eat with your workers, follow three important guidelines.

1) Eat slowly

This meal is not about survival. It's about bonding with members of your team.

Don't put your head down and attack your meal like a lion devouring an antelope. Slow down. Enjoy dining with your team member. Relax, smile, and tell stories. The business world is all about speed. But social bonding takes time. Workers won't feel like important members of your team if you invite them to lunch and then rush through it. As Stephen Covey famously said, when it comes to people: fast is slow and slow is fast. If you try to rush the process you will end up getting no results. And nowhere is this truer than at the dinner table.

As a general rule, take about three breaths in between swallows of your food. Any less and the meal feels rushed. It feels like a task, not a pleasure. You only bring people into the Social Circle with experiences, so make it a positive experience. Also, schedule sufficient blocks of time to share a meal. It's difficult to establish a bond over a five-minute snack. Give yourself at least thirty minutes to eat a proper meal. That provides enough time to harness the power of eating together without disrupting your schedule.

2) Use good manners

Shared meals are a potent way to bond with team members. But not in all circumstances. You can easily drive a teammate away. You can cause discomfort. You can present yourself as someone your workers wouldn't want to follow. And it all comes down to one simple factor: manners.

Manners are the behaviors that communicate politeness and courtesy. They are most relevant in social situations where physical functions take place. In the case of dining, it's the consumption of food. And manners help you to partake in this function without offending or causing discomfort in others. Simply put, manners help you eat with people without driving them away. And, as a leader, this is a must.

So follow basic manners when you eat. Chew with your mouth closed. Use your utensils properly. Maintain a neat and orderly plate. If you're not familiar with the guidelines of etiquette, then read a book on the topic. If you don't have good eating habits, then practice at home with a spouse or your children. Set aside one night every week to get out the fine china and practice good table manners. Develop the habits at home, so that they will feel natural with your teammates. Don't let bad manners alienate your workers and drive them out of the Social Circle. Be a leader that they want to break bread with.

3) Enjoy hearty laughter

Remember the firefighters. Their firehall meals were a time for laughing and good-natured teasing. It was a jovial environment. And this pleasant environment built the bonds that boosted performance.

Make your meals fun. Find opportunities to laugh. Tell jokes and funny stories. Laugh at the silly things that you observe. Comment with light-hearted chuckles. Develop a laugh-ready attitude and laugh whenever possible when people tell stories. The more you laugh together, the more bonding will occur. And the more they will feel like a part of your team.

Laughter doesn't have to happen all of the time. And you shouldn't try to force it. Simply create an environment where laughter comes easily. The best way to encourage laughter in others is to laugh yourself. That will set the tone and invite more laughter from your teammates. Laughter isn't just about humor.

It's social. It's not about being funny. It's about bonding. So just start laughing and other people will laugh along. As that happens, the bonds of teamwork will grow ever stronger.

As a final note, remember to eat with a positive mindset. When you share a meal, have a good attitude. Take pride in what you're accomplishing, and in what your team has done. While you eat your meal, bask in the glory of teamwork. Don't snipe or alienate your dining partners. That's counterproductive. Instead, act like a king, honored to be dining with your most loyal knights. Act like a lion. When they gather, it's called a pride.

CHAPTER SUMMARY

- Eating together is a primal way to reinforce team identity.
- Teams that eat together perform better than those that do not.
- Sharing a meal is one of the best ways to make someone who has felt excluded in the past feel included now.
- Eating guidelines when sharing a meal with your team include 1) eating slowly, 2) practicing good manners, and 3) laughing often.

ACTION ITEMS

- Brainstorm five ways that you can eat more often with the members of your team (for example, "Institute a monthly happy hour.").

  1. _____

  _____

2. _____

_____

3. _____

_____

4. _____

_____

5. _____

_____

- Brainstorm five funny stories (or jokes) that you can use to initiate laughter (for example, "The time that I got pulled over while delivering a mannequin murder scene to a movie studio.").

1. _____

_____

2. _____

_____

3. _____

_____

4. _____

_____

5. _____

_____

CHAPTER 23

SHARING THE PAIN

Eliminating the Leadership Shelter

M eals are fun and positive. They are a great way for your team to bond. And they demonstrate the potential of shared experiences. But arranging shared meals is not all you can do as a leader. You also need to harness negative experiences. Now we turn to the dark side— to a peculiar common experience that university administrators can't seem to eradicate.

On the surface of it, the practice seems primitive, ritualistic, and brutal. And yet it happens every year on college and university campuses across the USA.

The practice is called "hazing," and it occurs to young men who are pledging to join a college fraternity. It doesn't happen with every fraternity. And it happens in different forms and to varying degrees. But when it happens, it often looks like this.

A student, usually a freshman, applies to join an established fraternity on campus. But the student isn't accepted immediately. The student becomes a "pledge" alongside other freshman who also want to get in. Then, in addition to other demanding requirements, the fraternity members (older students) put the pledges through a series of deliberately uncomfortable experiences—anything from cleaning the house and running errands, to sleep deprivation and physical assault. And if the pledges can endure these experiences, then they are accepted and become full-fledged fraternity members. This process is called hazing, and the purpose is to humiliate and abuse the pledges. Most hazing behaviors are minor. But some abuse has been so extreme that it has caused permanent injuries and even death.[40]

So let's ask a simple question: Why do these hazing practices continue? Is it because fraternity members are predisposed to giving and receiving abuse? Unlikely. Is it because pledges have disproportionally low self-esteem? Probably not. And while there are likely many reasons that these rituals stubbornly persist, we would like to recognize one that's relevant to our discussion. It's a unique form of shared experience. The fraternity members have been through something that others have not. This creates a sense of social cohesion that wouldn't otherwise exist.

But what about the abuse? Why must they hurt and injure each other? It turns out that when people share a painful experience with each other, they naturally form bonds of camaraderie.

To test the truth of this, researchers ran a series of experiments.[41] In their first experiment, they put participants into small groups and assigned them a task. Participants submerged their hands into a water-filled container and moved a metal ball under the water. For the control, the water was lukewarm and produced no discomfort. But for the second group, the water was cold. Painfully cold. It caused agony for anyone who even just touched the water with their skin—much less held his hand underwater for a period of time to perform a task.

In other words, the participants in this group shared a painful experience.

Afterward, the participants rated their group experience. For example, they evaluated the extent to which they agreed with statements such as, "I feel part of this group experience," and, "I feel a sense of loyalty to other participants."

When the researchers compared these responses to those of the control group, they saw a stark difference. Those who worked in painfully cold water showed significantly higher levels of trust and feelings of camaraderie—and this held true even when taking into account race, age, gender, and other demographic factors. Think about what this means: the only difference was whether or not the groups had shared a painful experience. And when they had, they felt more like a team and felt more loyalty to their teammates than the people who had not.

The researchers described it as "social glue." When people share a painful experience, it acts as a type of glue that holds the team together. It provides a sense of commonality that makes people feel similar to—and familiar with—other people who went through the same experience. They feel like mutual allies who have been victimized by the same circumstances. And the researchers found this over and over again in their studies. In other experiments, they induced pain with physical exertion and by eating painfully hot chili peppers—and bonding between members of the group resulted in each.

In the words of the lead researcher, Brock Bastian, "Our findings show that pain is a particularly powerful ingredient in producing bonding and cooperation between those who share painful experiences….The findings shed light on why camaraderie may develop between soldiers or others who share difficult and painful experiences." In other words, shared pain alone helps to build social bonds.

This explains why otherwise decent fraternity members nevertheless ruthlessly haze a person that will soon become a close friend. He doesn't want to deny him the camaraderie that comes from sharing a painful experience.

Now, let's take a moment here to step back and establish some crucial boundaries. First, we do not advocate that anyone inflict pain on anyone without their consent—business, sports, and fraternity members included. We're just discussing a phenomenon that already exists. Don't manufacture hardship as a team-building exercise. Treat your people with respect and never inflict pain in any form on anybody. So then where does this leave us? If shared pain is powerful, but we shouldn't inflict pain, what can we do?

For the answer, let's learn from Teddy Roosevelt and his infamous Rough Riders.[42] During the Spanish-American war, Teddy was able to build a strong team from ordinary misfits in a remarkably short period. And with this group of volunteer soldiers, he charged Kettle Hill, winning fame and glory.

Afterwards, people often asked Roosevelt how he had built such a strong team in such a short period of time. He chose a fascinating example to explain it: wartime rationing.

"One reason we never had the slightest trouble in the regiment was because, when we got down to hard pan, officers and men shared exactly alike. It is alright to have differences in food and the like in times of peace and plenty, when everybody is comfortable. But in really hard times officers and men must share alike if the best work is to be done. As long as I had nothing but two hardtacks, which was the allowance to each man on the morning of the San Juan fight, no one could complain..."

In other words, when times got tough, he didn't shield himself from the pain—even though as a leader, he could have. Instead, he chose to experience the very same hardship that his men did. Do you see the difference? He didn't go out of his way to inflict pain on others. He just didn't shield himself, either. He didn't protect himself while his team suffered. They all suffered together. And this unlocked the power of shared pain.

You can do the same thing.

So how might this look? It's simple. If your team experiences hardship, check to see whether or not you are suffering to the same degree. If not, consider joining them. For example, imagine that you work in an office, and the whole team needs to stay late. What's going to happen if they have to stay late but you get to go home early? You're going to put distance between you and your team. And they are going to disengage from you a little. Furthermore, you will miss an opportunity to build strong bonds.

So if they stay late and it is practical for you to do so, then stay, too. If your construction crew has to wear uncomfortable safety equipment, then wear it yourself, too. Don't give yourself a free pass. Share in the pain that your people have to endure. Nothing else will send a more powerful message to them that you are all in it together.

CHAPTER SUMMARY

- Shared pain is a powerful source of team bonding.
- You can accelerate team building when you suffer alongside of your team.
- You should never artificially introduce a painful experience for the sake of team building.

ACTION ITEMS

- List five ways that you are shielded (or are shielding yourself) from the suffering of your team and state how you can establish equality:

Your Protection	Equality
Example: A special parking spot shields you from parking headaches	*Park with everyone else*

1. _____

   _____

   _____

2. _____

   _____

   _____

3. _____

   _____

   _____

4. _____

   _____

   _____

5. _____

   _____

   _____

CHAPTER 24

MOTIVATING SCROOGE

Showing the Social Consequences

You built your team and then you cemented it together with shared experiences. Now you need to bind your team even closer together. You must fulfill step three of the Social Circle. It's time to establish social responsibility. And to get started, let's travel back to Victorian England and meet the most socially unmotivated man on Christmas.

Ebenezer Scrooge didn't want to make friends.

As the main character from Charles Dickens's novel *A Christmas Carol*,[43] Scrooge was resistant to social bonding. He denied fundraisers who ask him to donate to the community. He denied his nephew's request to attend a Christmas party. But most of all, he refused to bond with his employee, Bob Cratchit—refusing to join him in Christmas merriment, lecturing him for his foolishness, and otherwise abusing him in the office.

Scrooge viewed himself as an island. And he saw Cratchit as an employee—something of a stranger—not a teammate. They spent lots of time together in the office, and they both suffered through the same cold weather. But Scrooge kept their relationship strictly transactional, paying Cratchit for his work and otherwise maintaining distance. And this prevented any social bonds from developing.

It seemed that nothing would motivate Scrooge to bond with his team member. But then, something strange occurred on Christmas Eve.

That evening, the Ghosts of Christmas visited Scrooge and took him on a journey. Each showed him a different vision of life and the consequences of his attitude of isolation. But perhaps none was so powerful as the vision shown to him by the Ghost of Christmas Present.

The Ghost of Christmas Present took Scrooge across town, to the holiday celebration of Bob Cratchit's family. Scrooge learned about Bob Cratchit's sickly son—Tiny Tim—who would die without proper medical treatment. But Cratchit can't afford it, making the chances of Tim's survival small. Scrooge took pity on the boy. And for the first time, he sees that his own treatment of Bob Cratchit affects more than his own profits. It affects Bob Cratchit enormously. And it's a matter of life and death for poor Tiny Tim.

This affects Scrooge deeply. The next morning, Scrooge is a changed man. He anonymously sends the Crachits a large turkey for Christmas dinner. He gives Bob Cratchit a much deserved raise. And he becomes a second father to Tiny Tim, financing the medical care that he desperately needs.

The story of Ebenezer Scrooge is one of dramatic transformation. And perhaps his greatest transformation came in the realm of social bonding. On Christmas Eve, he refused social bonds and deliberately alienated his team member. But on Christmas Day, he visited Cratchit's home, embraced him, and brought him gifts.

What brought about this change? He learned the consequences that his actions had on his teammates. He learned of

Tiny Tim, and the struggles facing the Cratchit family. He felt the social responsibility of his actions. This brought him into the Social Circle and pushed him up Köhler's Cone.

This illustrates an important feature of the Köhler effect. People perform at a higher level when they see how their performance affects others on their team. Scrooge gave Cratchit a raise and paid for Tiny Tim's medical expenses once he understood the child's struggles. That's what people tend to do. They give more once they see how others depend on them.

Researchers tested this principle among hospital workers.

Hospitals are notoriously dangerous as a place where one can easily catch infections. For example, in the US, one out of every twenty-five hospitalized patients contracts an infection.[44] But much of this could be avoided if health care professionals practiced better hygiene at work. So researchers conducted a study about how to motivate hospital workers to improve their hygiene.[45]

Their experiment was simple. They placed signs next to the hand sanitation dispensers. Then they weighed the bags at the beginning of their experiment and then weighed them again after two weeks. The bag that weighed the least indicated that more people had used that dispenser to clean themselves than other dispensers. In other words, a lighter bag meant better hygiene.

The researchers wanted to know which words displayed on the sign would lead to better hygiene. They tested three different types of signs.

The first concerned the health of the worker. It read:
1. HAND HYGIENE PREVENTS YOU FROM CATCHING DISEASES.
The second concerned the health of the patients. It read:
2. HAND HYGIENE PREVENTS PATIENTS FROM CATCHING DISEASES.

The third was the control which simply read:
3. GEL IN, WASH OUT.

So what was the result? The sign aimed at personal health made no impact. But the sign that appealed to the well-being of the patients proved vastly more effective. In the words of the researchers, "The amount of hand-hygiene product used from dispensers with the patient-consequences sign was significantly greater than the amount used from dispensers with the personal-consequences sign...or the control sign."

They repeated the experiment, but this time they spied on the hygiene station rather than weighing the bags. Again, the sign aimed at personal health made no impact. But the patient-focused sign created a 10 percent jump in hand-washing, particularly among physicians. When the sign reminded people about the dangers of patient infection, they were motivated to spend some extra time washing their hands.

What did Scrooge and these hospital workers have in common? When they didn't see beyond their own bubble, they didn't see any reason to inconvenience themselves for others. But when they realized the impact of their behavior on others—people that they cared for—they made a change.

How did this happen? Did Scrooge do it on his own?

No. He needed the help of the Christmas ghosts. They came and showed him something that he hadn't realized before. They showed him the consequences of his actions on his teammate. It was the same in the hospital. Health care workers were willing to wash their hands in order to protect the patients. But when they didn't think about their patients—when their thoughts were on other things—they weren't motivated to go the extra distance.

This is your job as a leader. You can't just put people on a team and expect them to automatically understand how their performance impacts their teammates. It may be obvious for Olympic swimmers, but it's rarely so clear in a business setting.

Consider a staff accountant who works for a small marketing company. His job is to complete the week's paperwork every Friday before going home. And he usually leaves work at precisely 5:00 p.m. EST. But suppose a salesman is closing a deal in a PST zone. He won't be able to get the paperwork to the accountant before 5:00 p.m. And if the accountant goes home at 5:00 p.m. like he always does, then the salesman won't be able to file the paperwork and meet his sales quota, thus putting his job at risk.

What's going to happen in this situation? Will the Köhler effect activate, causing the accountant to stay late and file the paperwork before the deadline? Not if the accountant does not understand the consequences of his actions. Without knowing how his behavior impacts the other members of his team, he won't be motivated to change it. He will leave at 5:00 p.m. like he always does, unwittingly leaving his teammate stranded. But if he knows, then everything will be different. He will feel the Social Circle and the Köhler effect will activate.

This is where you come in. You can help the accountant understand the situation. Tell him about the salesman's schedule. Or create a system of communicating his travel schedule—maybe a travel calendar posted above the place where the accountant files paperwork. You've got to spread the information around the team. And you've got to make it clear how everyone's performance affects each other.

Scrooge can't pay for Tiny Tim's medical expenses without knowing that he's sick. Physicians don't feel motivated to wash their hands unless they're reminded about the consequences for their patients. And your people won't give an extraordinary performance until they understand how their behavior affects their teammates.

Show your workers how everyone on the team depends on each other. This establishes social responsibility and binds the team together. This is the true foundation of the Social Circle. And it's the energizing force behind the Köhler effect.

CHAPTER SUMMARY

- People work harder when they understand how their performance affects others.
- Workers don't automatically understand how their performance has consequences for their teammates.
- Leaders can help their teammates make connections between what they do and how others are affected.

ACTION ITEMS

- Identify five tasks that are difficult to see the consequences of (for example, "Quality control workers may not see how they save the accountants the paperwork required of product recalls.").

1. _____

   _____

2. _____

   _____

3. _____

_____

4. _____

_____

5. _____

_____

- List five ways to help workers see how their performance affects their teammates (for example, "Bring quality control workers into an accounting meeting during a product recall.").

1. _____

_____

2. _____

_____

3. _____

_____

4. _____

_____

5. _____

_____

CHAPTER 25

THE PEAK TASK

Turning Workers into Leaders

We've reached the final technique of the Social Circle. And this one is the most important. It brings people to the very center of the the circle and to the very top of the triangle. It makes people feel socially indispensable. And leaders can never achieve greatness until they master it.

Let's let a modern-day hero show us how she does it.

Dr. Mimi Silbert does the impossible. She rehabilitates hardened criminals. Through her organization, the Delancey Street Foundation, she has taken in over fourteen thousand former convicts, gang members, and drug addicts—helping change their lives and find them a productive role in society.[46]

Needless to say, this is quite a challenge. And yet she has succeeded remarkably well. She reports that, of the tens of thousands that have gone through her program, more than 90 percent never return to drugs or crime. Think about that. She takes the worst of worst—people typically come to her with four felonies—and she helps them put their pasts behind them. They get clean, get a job, and utterly change their lives.

Her success has been so impressive that people have come from far and wide to learn how she does it. And she explains her success in simple terms. She puts the people who need help on a team with mutual responsibility and mutual accountability. And she moves them through the team responsibilities quickly.

Here's how it works. When people enter her program, she immediately puts them on a crew doing jobs such as moving furniture or setting tables at a restaurant. The new workers receive a mentor (another ex-convict), who explains and demonstrates how to do the job. So the new workers immediately feel the Köhler effect activate. The day they walk in the door, the members of their new team depend on their performance for the whole team's success.

Then something interesting happens. As quickly as possible, usually after only a week on the job, the new worker becomes a mentor to someone else—an even more recent recruit who has just enrolled in the program. Now our original worker is responsible for explaining the rules and showing the new worker how to perform the tasks. In other words, as quickly as possible, the former criminals who enroll at Delancey are given leadership roles!

This quickly weaves a worker into the fabric of the team. Why? Because not only does a person have a task to do; now they also have the responsibility of passing it on to the people entering the program. They become leaders who oversee the activity of their team members. The newer recruits depend on their mentors guide them on how to behave in their new environment.

The worker-turned-leader immediately feels a strong identification with the team. And this is strong enough to help the ex-convicts resist the temptation to quit the program and return to a life of crime. They feel sufficiently included on the team to leave their old identities behind. And this starts happening after the first week of enrollment in the program. That's the power that a leadership position has on team self-identification.

This is the highest form of delegation: the delegation of leadership. It's powerful to assign someone a task. That's a necessary action to bring them onto the team. But it's even more powerful to give a person a leadership role. That makes them feel like they are in the inner circle, that their actions help to hold the team together. And that's true! When you assign leadership to others, they influence the identity and direction of the team. So when you delegate the power of leadership, you bring people more deeply into the fold.

Seasoned managers in the professional world recognize this. Some of their workers teeter on the fence. They have demonstrated their competence, but they don't yet feel loyal to the team. They don't feel the camaraderie of the Social Circle. And they have one foot out of the door, ready to leave for the competition at any moment. Seasoned managers know that they face a choice: promote them, or lose them. They either give these workers a leadership position, or the workers will find positions elsewhere.

If you've ever felt this pressure in your own career, then you know the consequences of leadership. Leadership positions make people feel necessary and needed. It makes them feel important and valuable. And it anchors them onto their team, addressing both aspects of Köhler's Cone. It's the most motivational thing you can give your workers.

So how can you use this motivational tool?

1) Give away the easy leadership
Don't feel that you have to be in charge of every job just because you are a leader. Some things are easy to lead—such as things

that are routine, familiar, and well understood. Let somebody else lead those. That will build a sense of community and importance among the new leaders.

Give someone else the responsibility to assign and oversee the work. For example, suppose you typically schedule work shifts for the factory floor. It's routine and familiar, but it's nevertheless important. You might delegate this task to one of your workers—perhaps a factory worker. All of sudden, that worker doesn't feel like a fringe member of the company any more. Now he feels like a part of the team. And his loyalty and motivation will increase.

2) Tap into current competence

Empower people to lead where they have expertise. At Delancey Street Foundation, the tasks aren't complicated. It doesn't take long to learn how to set a table. And once the participants have learned how to do the task, Dr. Silbert immediately gives them a leadership role. Follow her example. Motivate workers by getting them to teach others the things that they already know.

Consider a grandfather. As he ages, he might find that his family has started to downgrade his role. And this makes him feel like less of a member of the family. But what if his son asks him to teach the grandchildren a skill, such as how to fish? Then the grandfather will get to pass on his knowledge. He will feel valuable again. He will matter to the family.

So tap into the skills and wisdom that your people already have. Give them an opportunity to share that wisdom with others. It doesn't have to be all of the time, and you don't need to grant formal titles. But get everybody to play a leadership or mentorship role. It's a great way to spread the skills throughout a team and make everyone feel more valuable.

3) Prepare workers for leadership

Several years ago, we gave a workshop for a company that was trying to expand. And we emphasized the necessity of delegation and preparing others to lead. During the workshop, a manager spoke up. He wasn't on the company's executive team, but he was the highest-ranking person in the room, and was responsible for overseeing all of the others. And he said:

> *"We need to be doing more of this. When I was in the military, everyone was trained to do the job of two positions above them, and one position below. We learned that the hard way. Because in war, things change quickly and people often need to be replaced in the line of fire. So it was a matter of survival to train soldiers for leadership. That's how you win the war. And if we want to win in business, if we want to initiate the growth that we're talking about, then we need to do the same thing."*

We never forgot that. The United States military learned that lesson the hard way. If you want to win the war, then you have to prepare people for leadership. The average people. The ordinary people. You need to prepare them for leadership in advance of their promotion. You have to invest in your people and train them to lead, putting them in progressively higher leadership positions.

Make no mistake—formal delegation is not the only way that this works. It works any time that one person on a team depends on another for guidance about a task. You can set up mentorship relationships or designate team members to train others, acting as a source of knowledge about particular jobs. This makes people feel both included in the team and valued as an important member.

At the Delancey Street Foundation, Dr. Silbert teaches us that leadership is a tool of change and transformation. We should bring people onto the team while their commitment is uncertain, and then set them onto a new path to reengage their motivation. This ability to turn your team members into leaders is the litmus test for your effectiveness as a leader. Poor leaders are those who have no followers. Average leaders are those who lead a team of followers. But extraordinary leaders are those who lead a team of leaders! There's no greater mark of success than leading a team of highly competent and highly loyal leaders.

You can be a great leader. You can develop your team into a highly competent group of leaders. And there's no better time to start than right now.

CHAPTER SUMMARY

- Leadership assignments address both dimensions of Köhler's Cone.
- People are often ready for leadership before you realize they are.
- When workers share their wisdom with the next generation of workers, they feel irreplaceable.
- The three ways to empower leadership are 1) give away the easy leadership, 2) tap into current competence, and 3) prepare workers for leadership.
- Leadership empowerment can be either formal or informal.

ACTION ITEMS

- List five leadership tasks that you can assign to others, specifying the formality of the assignment and who will receive the task.

The Leadership

Task	Formality	Person
Example: Scheduling weekend work assignments	*Formal*	*Crystal Nguyen*

1. _____

_____

_____

2. _____

_____

_____

3. _____

_____

_____

4. _____

_____

_____

5. _____

_____

_____

CHAPTER 26

HIT THE GROUND RUNNING

Taking the First Steps

I t's time to get started. No more theory. No more discussion. It's time to actually apply the ideas of this book to your working model and answer the call to higher leadership.

When we coach leaders, we craft a customized program for them to follow—a plan tailored to the specifics of their circumstances. But lacking this, don't wait to embark on your journey. You need to take action. You need to get started.

Here is a quick-start game plan. It's something that you can do the moment you put down this book. It's a way to put these ideas into action immediately. Follow these four steps, and you will be well on your way to the leadership push.

1) Start a file for each person you want to motivate

This is the most basic step, but it's where everything starts. You can't trigger a massive improvement in people accidentally. You can't drift your way to the top of a mountain. It needs to be deliberate. It needs to be professional.

Create a file for the motivation of your team. This will be your headquarters of activity and planning. We call these "push files." Here, you will organize the information you have on your workers. Start by making a list of everyone you want to motivate.

Then create a simple push file for each person, beginning with just the basic facts—such as their position, their history, etc. And if someone new comes onto your team or someone from outside it requires a motivational boost, then create push files for them, too.

This is how it might look: it comes to your attention that an employee is underperforming and needs some inspirational motivation. So you sit down at your desk and open his push file—it could be either an electronic file or a paper file. For this example, let's assume it's a paper file. You write the name of your worker on the tab of the file folder, "John Doe." And on a piece of paper, you record all of the information about Mr. Doe's position, experience, duration with the company, and anything else that seems relevant. Then you put the paper in the folder and put the push file away. But you reach for it often. You review it before meetings or before delegating assignments to Mr. Doe. Whenever an issue with Mr. Doe arises, you first consult his file and reacquaint yourself with the information you have about him. This keeps you apprised of Mr. Doe's motivational progress over time.

The basic idea is to create a baseline for your future motivational efforts. And you need to feel comfortable using the push file. It's of no use if it gets lost in the back of a cabinet somewhere, never to be seen again. You need to use your push file and refer to it often. Get comfortable opening it and referencing the information that it contains. At first, there won't be much to reference. But that will begin to change with step two.

2) Observe their behavior

A file isn't valuable until it contains information. And that's true for push files. Once you have created one, you need to fill it with data. You achieve that data through observation.

Watch your people as they work throughout the day. Watch what they do and listen to what they say. Over time, people will reveal themselves. They will expose their values and lay bare their opinions. Some people speak with words, and others through actions. But all people eventually reveal their values. You cannot hide from observation.

Your job is to observe your team members' behavior and record what you see. You don't need to record everything—just that which is relevant to your goal. Remember, your goal is to push people up Köhler's Cone. So record information that's relevant to both the Task Triangle and the Social Circle. Over time, this will indicate their position on Köhler's Cone, telling you which element to focus on and what will be most difficult for them to grasp.

This is how it might look: after a meeting, you overhear John Doe tell a coworker that the team project "seems pointless" and is a "waste of time." When you return to your desk, you pull out your push file on John Doe and open it. On a form called "journal," you log the date of the incident, and write, "After the Monday meeting, John told a coworker that the project was pointless." Then you record what this indicates about his position on the cone. "This suggests that John considers the job to be low on the Task Triangle." Then you put the journal back and close the file.

3) Develop motivation scripts

Information isn't valuable until it influences action. This is true of the information you gather during your observations. You need to use that information to help the people that you want to motivate. Your records will help you tailor specific and useful strategies to help them. This will make their improvement more likely.

At this point, your job is to assemble motivational scripts that apply to the worker's situation. These are the phrases you should plan to use in conversation in response to their behavior. And when people behave in ways to indicate a particular position on Köhler's Cone, you'll be prepared to contribute a motivational message.

This is how the scenario might look. You sit at your desk when you have a spare moment. And you pull out John Doe's push file. You review the journal entries indicating that he is low on Köhler's Cone. He thinks the project is pointless. So you pull out a blank script form and write five things you can say to bring him up the Task Triangle. You like the way the third one sounds, so you put a star next to it: "John, when you work on this project, you're affecting a lot of people. It's not a meaningless task. You're helping patients to get the medical care they need. This helps them return to work and provide for their families. Even though you may not see it, there are a lot of people who depend on you." Then you review how John usually expresses cynicism after the Monday meeting. So you practice your script aloud several times and prepare to use it next Monday if John calls the project pointless.

Practice your scripts and prepare to deliver them at the proper moment. This will probably require you to improve your speaking habits. It's likely that you have some negative habits that you use when the pressure is high. For example, you may have a tendency to point the finger when you don't see the results you want. This was Lisa's mistake in Chapter 6. And until she broke this habit, she wasn't able to motivate her team members.

You need to eliminate these negative habits. You need to replace them with positive, constructive phrases. And you need to elevate your general patterns of speech. So make a list of negative scripts that you use. Be honest with yourself. If possible, ask a trusted friend or colleague to help you identify these negative habits. Others often see you more clearly than you see yourself. And they can help identify your blindspots. Once you have your list of negative scripts in hand, replace each with a positive script on the corresponding dimension of the Köhler's Cone.

For example, suppose you recognize that you often use the phrase, "Fine! I'll just do it myself! I'm the only one who pulls my weight around here anyway!" This phrase probably discourages the Köhler effect among your teammates. You need to eliminate that script and replace it with something better. So write the original script on a piece of paper and next to it write a positive replacement. For example, you might write, "Look, I know it's difficult. But no one here can do it alone. We need you to give your best. We either win together, or we all lose separately." Practice this new script aloud several times. And every time you feel tempted to use the old script, initiate the positive one instead. As you make this new script a habit, you will inspire more motivation from your people. But for this to work, this replacement needs to be planned and practiced in advance. That will allow you to depend on your new habits when the pressure is on.

At this step, you now have two lists. First, you have a list of phrases and actions that you have observed from your people— things that indicate their position on Köhler's Cone. And next to each of these phrases or actions you have a preplanned script that you can use in response.

Second, you have a list of negative phrases or actions that you have used in the past—things that have discouraged motivation from your people. And next to each item on this list, you have written out a replacement phrase to use. As you practice these positive scripts, using them will become a natural reflex.

With these two lists in hand, you'll be well on your way to fulfilling your leadership potential. But both of these lists are somewhat reactive and passive. The final step in your game plan is proactive.

4) Plan frequent, inspirational interactions

If you want to elicit extraordinary motivation from someone, it's not enough just to decide to do it. It's not enough to observe them and record their patterns. And it's not enough to change your speech patterns and respond to them with motivational language. These things are all necessary, and they build on each other, but they are not enough. You need to be proactive.

Plan opportunities to meet individually with the people that you want to motivate. Make room for their motivational growth in your work schedule. Don't just hope that they will climb Köhler's Cone by themselves. You need to push them. Don't just wait around for a convenient opportunity to let them know they're valued to present itself. Give people preplanned, one-on-one time. Deliberately get together when it otherwise would not happen. Schedule motivational interactions so that you can monitor their performance and address their concerns more closely. Think of it like a physician's regular checkup, or like preventative maintenance on your car. To keep people motivated, you need to give them regular doses of your time and attention.

This is how it might look: you sit down at your desk and look at your calendar. It's pretty crowded. But you see that you have an opening next Thursday during your lunch hour. So you send an email to John Doe, inviting him to join you for lunch. In your notes, you remind yourself to talk with John about the big-picture importance of both his job and the project as a whole. Then you set reminders on your calendar to notify you every month to schedule an encouraging, inspirational meeting with John. And you write a quick list of ideas of what these future meetings might look like: "eat lunch together, carpool to a conference together, play golf together, etc."

These meetings are not formal performance reviews. Strictly speaking, you are not reviewing a worker's performance at all. You are reviewing their thoughts, attitude, and motivation. You are checking their position on Köhler's Cone. And you respond to them not with threats or formal authority, but with conversation and planned inspirational scripts. These meetings are all about the attitudes that motivate their performance.

One final note: the consistency of your attention matters more than the intensity of your efforts. Resist the temptation to schedule one meeting and try to push people all the way up Köhler Cone immediately. Don't flood them with information and don't lecture them on how they should be thinking. Focus on bite-size inspirations that they receive consistently. A little bit at a time works far better than massive lectures that happen only occasionally. Commit to the growth of your people. And commitment is best expressed through consistency.

This completes your quick-start game plan. With this plan in hand, you can bring all of the knowledge and research of this book to bear on your position as a leader. You will motivate your ordinary workers to extraordinary performance through the Köhler effect.

CHAPTER SUMMARY

- Nothing will change unless you start taking new actions.
- Your leadership file is the key to your improvement.
- Use your leadership scripts, and your people will respond.

ACTION CHECKLIST

- Mark the box once you have assembled all the elements of your leadership file

  - A file for each person you want to motivate ☐

  - An observation journal in each file ☐

  - A collection of five+ motivation scripts in each file ☐

  - A list of frequent interactions planned for the next twelve months ☐

CHAPTER 27

THE EXPERIENCE OF A LIFETIME

Finding Meaning beyond Business

We've been on quite a journey together.

Our goal was not to make this book as long as possible. We tossed aside earlier versions of it that were twice as long. Instead, we wanted to create something short and focused that explored a single topic and that provided actionable advice. If you've made it this far, then we have accomplished both.

The Leadership Push is about one thing: how to motivate extraordinary performance from ordinary people. In Part I, we saw that this type of leadership requires a particular attitude. Before you do anything else, you need to develop the right mindset. You must have the ambition to be a great leader. You need to see yourself as an inspirational leader who can achieve impressive things with your people. Then you need to believe that extraordinary performance is possible. You must believe that great things come from small beginnings and you must fall in love with ordinary people. After all, as a leader they are both your source material and the only way you will achieve greatness.

In Part II we answered the riddle of motivation. How do you motivate extraordinary performance? You make people feel like important members of the team. You activate the Köhler effect through feelings of social indispensability. We discussed how the cone consists of two parts. One part is the Task Triangle, which measures how important a worker feels their work is to the team's shared goal. The other is the Social Circle, which measures how included a worker feels in the team. Put these two together, and you get Köhler's Cone. As people rise higher in the cone, they feel more needed, and more irreplaceable. This activates the Köhler effect and unleashes massive reservoirs of motivation.

In Part III we explored the Task Triangle, discussing actionable techniques that will make workers feel more important about their tasks. In Part IV we did something similar with the Social Circle, exploring techniques to make people feel connected and included in the team. Together, these methods bring the best out of your ordinary, everyday workers.

Now there is one last thing. We need to remind you that you, too, are irreplaceable.

As a leader, you are in a position to dramatically impact the lives of your workers. You can either encourage them to work, grow, and confront obstacles with a determined smile. Or you can let them settle into a routine and slowly stagnate. You can help them achieve ever-larger goals. Or you can make them feel alienated from the team each time they commit an error. You will set the atmosphere for your team, and that alone will influence the course of their lives. Being part of, and contributing to, a great team is one of the most rewarding experiences that a person will ever have. It can be a life-changing experience.

At first, this caught us off guard. We assumed that work was a means to an end. People showed up and punched the clock. They had no interest in team dynamics. They were just working to put food on the table and educate their children, both of which fully justify the effort.

But throughout our coaching and corporate training, the nonbusiness rewards of teamwork kept emerging. We would ask people about a positive team that they enjoyed being a part of in the past, and their faces would immediately light up. The team might have been a sports team they played on in high school, or a ragtag sales team they were a part of early in their career. And when people spoke of these experiences, they wouldn't only talk about the money they made or the success they achieved. They would also talk about the thrill of being on a dynamic team. They would talk about the adventure and uncertainty that brought them all together. They would talk about how their spouses and family members all spent time with other team members' spouses and family members. How everyone was a mutual ally that could be trusted completely. How each worker felt needed. And how sad they felt when the team disbanded. They used the language of the Köhler effect, not concerning motivational gains, but concerning the quality of life that it had provided!

We've encountered this over and over throughout the years. Managers who reminisce about their early careers when they belonged to some other leader's exciting team. Workers who feel lethargic in their current team in comparison to the energizing team that had its heyday years before. Retirees who still attend reunions of a team they belonged to decades earlier. Teams matter to people. A good team is one of the great treasures in life.

And the memories gained from membership on such a team can rank among the very best memories a person can have!

This is what you can create. This is within your power as a leader. Not only to create this experience for your workers but also for yourself as well!

Follow the techniques concerning Köhler's Cone. Master them. Use them with all of your ordinary workers. And soon you will find a new buzz starting to form—a new electricity in the atmosphere. Keep going. Keep making the effort. And soon you will create that exciting team element—that adventuresome, electrifying team feeling that pushes people to do their best and give every last bit of energy they have. This is the team that will help you achieve great things. This is the team that will charge up Kettle Hill for you. This is that team that will run through brick walls for you. And it might even become a life-changing type of team—the type of team that people remember in their old age while they reflect on the joyous vitality of their youth.

You are the leader. You can make this happen. The rewards are staggering.

We invite you to take this journey.

Good luck.

ENDNOTES

1. Roosevelt, Theodore. Rough Riders (classic reprint). S.L.: Forgotten Books, 2015.
2. Brands, Henry William. TR: The Last Romantic (full biography). New York, NY: Basic Books, 1997.
3. Strock, James M. Theodore Roosevelt on leadership: executive lessons from the bully pulpit. New York, NY: Three Rivers Press, 2003.
4. Roosevelt, Theodore. *An Autobiography*. New York, NY: Macmillan, 1913.
5. "Strategic Circle: 2018 CEO Survey: Overview and Analysis," Bob Ramsey Seminars, 1/17/2018.
6. "Temple University." Acres of Diamonds | Temple University. Accessed January 24, 2018. https://www.temple.edu/about/history -and-traditions/acres-diamonds.
7. Cummins, John. Francis Drake: the lives of a hero. London: Phoenix, 1997.
8. Sir Francis Drake committed many immoral acts that we do not support. In particular, we condemn his participation in the slave trade. Although this was not the defining feature of his career, we want to clearly state that we do not support it. In this project, we are concerned more with Drake's motto than his life. But we take this opportunity to formally condemn all acts of racism, bigotry, and the initiation of force on others.
9. Chang, Kenneth. "Highest Honor in Mathematics Is Refused." The New York Times. August 21, 2006. Accessed January 24, 2018. http://www.nytimes.com/2006/08/22/science/22cnd-math.html.

10. Conte, Christian. "Nordstrom customer service tales not just legend." Bizjournals.com. Accessed January 24, 2018. https://www.bizjournals.com/jacksonville/blog/retail_radar/2012/09/nordstrom-tales-of-legendary-customer.html. This story was recounted by Erik Nordstrom, the president of stores at Nordstrom, at the July 2012 annual meeting.

11. Edwards, Jim. "Check Out The Insane Lengths Zappos Customer Service Reps Will Go To." Business Insider. January 09, 2012. Accessed January 24, 2018. http://www.businessinsider.com/zappos-customer-service-crm-2012-1.

12. "A Marriott Associate Who Gave 'The Pants Off His Legs'." Marriott on the Move. Accessed January 24, 2018. http://www.blogs.marriott.com/marriott-on-the-move/2009/04/a-marriott-associate-who-gave-the-pants-off-his-legs.html.

13. "Injured Kerri Strug vaults the U.S. to gymnastics gold." NY Daily News. July 23, 2015. Accessed January 24, 2018. http://www.nydailynews.com/sports/more-sports/kerri-stands-tall-sprained-ankle-article-1.2015138.

14. After the games, it was determined that the Americans had already clinched gold, regardless of Kerri Strug's second run. That means that she did not have to take her second win to secure the gold medal. However, this was not known to her at the time, nor to the coaches of the American team. So Strug felt the same pressure as if her second run was necessary.

15. "Florida Marlins 4, New York Yankees 3." Retrosheet Boxscore: Florida Marlins 4, New York Yankees 3. Accessed January 24, 2018. http://www.retrosheet.org/boxesetc/2003/B10220FLO2003.htm.

16. A coaching client for Bob Ramsey Seminars in 2011, name changed for anonymity

17. "Frequently asked questions." Habitat for Humanity. Accessed January 24, 2018. https://www.habitat.org/about/faq.

18. "Habitat for Humanity raises walls on its 800,000th milestone home." Habitat for Humanity. Accessed January 24, 2018. https://www.habitat.org/newsroom/11-06-2013-800k-milestone.

19. Taken from the author's personal experience, volunteering in Terrebonne Parish Louisiana in 2009 and taking the leadership

development program in 2010 hosted by St. Louis Community College—Forest Park Campus.

20. Köhler, Otto. "Kraftleistungen bei Einzel- und Gruppenabeit [Physical performance in individual and group situations]." *Industrielle Psychotechnik*, 3, (1926): 274–282.

21. Köhler, Otto. "Über den Gruppenwirkungsgrad der menschlichen Körperarbeit und die Bedingung optimaler Kollektivkraftreaktion [On group efficiency of physical labor and the conditions of optimal collective performance]." *Industrielle Psychotechnik*, 4, (1927): 209–226.

22. Irwin, Brandon. "If You Want to Motivate Someone, Shut Up Already." Harvard Business Review. July 31, 2014. Accessed January 25, 2018. https://hbr.org/2013/07/if-you-want-to-motivate-someone-shut-up-already.

23. Hüffmeier, Joachim, Stefan Krumm, Jens Kanthak, and Guido Hertel. "'Dont let the group down': Facets of instrumentality moderate the motivating effects of groups in a field experiment." *European Journal of Social Psychology* 42, no. 5 (2012): 533–38. doi:10.1002/ejsp.1875.

24. Lisa Dillman | Times Staff Writer. "A team player who rises to the challenge." Los Angeles Times. August 12, 2008. Accessed January 25, 2018. http://articles.latimes.com/2008/aug/12/sports/sp-olylezak12.

25. Hüffmeier, Joachim, Jens Kanthak, and Guido Hertel. „Specificity of partner feedback as moderator of group motivation gains in Olympic swimmers." *Group Processes & Intergroup Relations* 16, no. 4 (2012): 516–25. doi:10.1177/1368430212460894.

26. Taken from the author's experience, volunteering in Terrebonne Parish Louisiana, 2009.

27. *The Holy Bible.* London: Collins, 2011. Genesis 11:1–9; Nyelvo Kbmroc mbyccoc Loxdvkgo.

28. In this book, we use the terms "abstraction" and "concept" interchangeably, while contrasting each against the "concrete," "specific," and/or "particular." We consider a concept to be the quality of an object considered independently of its specific features. For example, you may consider the redness of a strawberry,

a cardinal, and a firetruck. Redness is a quality that they all share. To consider redness independently is to form an abstraction. Concepts can be created from other concepts, increasing in rank—for example, a lion is at the same time a cat, a mammal, and an animal. For more information, refer to an introductory book on epistemology.

29. Bechky, Beth Allison. "Crossing occupational boundaries: Communication and learning on a production floor." PhD diss., Stanford University, 1999.

30. Ross, Lee, Richard E. Nisbett, and Malcolm Gladwell. The person and the situation: perspectives of social psychology. London: Pinter & Martin, 2011.

31. Fandt, Patricia M. "The Relationship of Accountability and Interdependent Behavior to Enhancing Team Consequences." Group & Organization Studies 16, no. 3 (1991): 300–12. doi:10.1177/105960119101600305.

32. Taken from experience with a client of Bob Ramsey Seminars, Kansas USA, 2011.

33. Ambrose, Stephen E. Citizen soldiers: the U.S. Army from the Normandy beaches to the surrender of Germany. London: Simon & Schuster, 2016.

34. Walton, Greg, Priyanka B. Carr, and Lauren C. Howe. "Cues of working together fuel intrinsic motivation and can contribute to the solution of collective action problems." PsycEXTRA Dataset. doi:10.1037/e578192014-274.

35. Harris, Christopher M., Gary C. Mcmahan, and Patrick M. Wright. "Talent and time together." Personnel Review 41, no. 4 (2012): 408–27. doi:10.1108/00483481211229357.

36. Fiske, Susan T., Amy J.C. Cuddy, and Peter Glick. "Universal dimensions of social cognition: warmth and competence." Trends in Cognitive Sciences 11, no. 2 (2007): 77–83. doi:10.1016/j.tics.2006.11.005.

37. Gottman, John Mordechai. The mathematics of marriage: Dynamic nonlinear models. MIT Press, 2005.

38. Kniffin, Kevin M., Brian Wansink, Carol M. Devine, and Jeffery Sobal. "Eating Together at the Firehouse: How Workplace Commensality Relates to the Performance of Firefighters." *Human Performance* 28, no. 4 (2015): 281–306. doi:10.1080/08959285.2015.1021049.

39. Hofferth, Sandra L., and John F. Sandberg. "How American Children Spend Their Time." *Journal of Marriage and Family* 63, no. 2 (2001): 295–308. doi:10.1111/j.1741-3737.2001.00295.x.

40. Ganim, Sara. "Court rules against Penn State in two fraternity hazing lawsuits." CNN. May 31, 2017. Accessed January 25, 2018. http://www.cnn.com/2017/05/30/us/penn-state-frat-hazing-rulings/index.html.

41. Bastian, Brock, Jolanda Jetten, and Laura J. Ferris. "Pain as Social Glue." *Psychological Science* 25, no. 11 (2014): 2079–085. doi:10.1177/0956797614545886.

42. Roosevelt, Theodore. *An Autobiography*. New York, NY: Macmillan, 1913.

43. Dickens, Charles. A Christmas carol: in prose, being a ghost story of Christmas. Edinburgh: Barrington Stoke, 2017.

44. Bernstein, Lenny. "One in 25 patients has an infection acquired during hospital stay, CDC says." The Washington Post. March 26, 2014. Accessed January 26, 2018. https://www.washingtonpost.com/news/to-your-health/wp/2014/03/26/one-in-25-patients-has-an-infection-acquired-during-hospital-stay-cdc-says/?utm_term=.fd5e130aaf4f.

45. Grant, Adam M., and David A. Hofmann. "It's Not All About Me." *Psychological Science* 22, no. 12 (2011): 1494–499. doi:10.1177/0956797611419172.

46. Grenny, Joseph, and Kerry Patterson. *Influencer: the power to change anything*. New York: McGraw-Hill Professional, 2013.